THE HONOURS SYSTEM

By the same author:

ELGAR: THE MAN
DENTON WELCH: THE MAKING OF A WRITER
THE JOURNALS OF DENTON WELCH *(Edited)*

THE HONOURS SYSTEM

Michael De-la-Noy

ALLISON & BUSBY
LONDON · NEW YORK

First published in Great Britain 1985 by
Allison & Busby Ltd,
6a Noel Street, London W1V 3RB

Copyright © Michael De-la-Noy 1985

British Library Cataloguing in Publication Data
De-la-Noy, Michael
　The honours system.
　1. Decorations of honor — Great Britain
　I. Title
　929.7'2　　　CR4801

ISBN 0-85031-614-6

Set in 11/12½ pt Sabon by Ann Buchan (Typesetters),
Walton-on-Thames, Surrey
Printed and bound in Great Britain by
The Camelot Press Ltd
Shirley Road, Southampton

For all my friends who have made it to the top, not forgetting those who were born there

The princes of Europe have found out a manner of rewarding their subjects who have behaved well, by presenting them with about two yards of blue ribbon, which is worn about the shoulder. They who are honoured by this mark of distinction are called knights, and the king himself is always the head of the order. This is a very frugal method of recompensing the most important services; and it is very fortunate for kings that their subjects are satisfied with such trifling rewards. Should a nobleman happen to lose a leg in battle, the king presents him with two yards of ribbon, and he is paid for the loss of his limb. Should an ambassador spend all his paternal fortune in supporting the honour of his country abroad, the king presents him with two yards of ribbon, which is to be considered as an equivalent to his estate. In short, while a European king has a yard of blue or green ribbon left, he need be under no apprehension of wanting statesmen, generals, and soldiers.

OLIVER GOLDSMITH: *Happiness and Show*

Contents

Introduction		9
The Principal British Honours		15
Glossary		17
CHAPTER ONE:	"A Greate Heart's Ease"	19
CHAPTER TWO:	Lords and Ladies	37
CHAPTER THREE:	Second-Class Peers	53
CHAPTER FOUR:	Knights and Dames	63
CHAPTER FIVE:	"A Sorry Ambition"	85
CHAPTER SIX:	Maundy Gregory	105
CHAPTER SEVEN:	Who Gets What . . .	123
CHAPTER EIGHT:	. . . and How	151
CHAPTER NINE:	Conclusions	167
Books Consulted		183
Index		185

Introduction

To disentangle and make plain every facet and social nuance of the British honours system would require the dedication to minutiae usually exhibited by the compiler of a handbook on etiquette combined with the scholarly precision of a professor of pure mathematics. The result, while no doubt proving to be both definitive and immaculately written, might nevertheless serve to direct the reader with only a general interest in the subject towards a more entertaining branch of literature; novels, poetry, biography all come to mind. For example, it is not enough, should it be your ambition to become a society hostess, to know that the daughter of a baron who marries a knight retains her style The Honourable; you will need to progress a step further to discover that should her husband be sent to the House of Lords she will drop it. And if you run a charity and want to address an appeal to a potential benefactor who won the DSO in the war and has since been made CBE and MVO, and you wish to know in which order to type this string of initials, you will — once again — not necessarily find the information you seek in this book.

What I *have* attempted to do is to place the origins of the honours system in their historical context, to demonstrate the social and political development of the system, in particular the way in which it has dominated, if not actually become synonymous with, militarism and governance, and to highlight some of the more bizarre, comical and scandalous episodes through which our modern and now largely respectable cascade of available honours has passed. In doing so, I have tried to make clear the sequence of events, but strict chronology is not one of the most notable attributes of the honours system in relation to the actual creation of certain titles and their current seniority in the order of precedence.

Today, peers rank from dukes down to marquesses, earls, viscounts and barons. Yet in terms of invention, dukes and marquesses came late on the scene, and then in very small numbers, while for many years after the Norman Conquest, barons superseded earls in importance. And while today we tend to think of all peerages created before the 1958 Life Peerage Act as being hereditary, succession to a peerage, like succession to the monarchy itself, was not in earliest times a foregone conclusion. Society at every level has been in far greater flux and for far longer than we often realize, and it is in fact only in comparatively recent times that the set of rules and regulations for governing the many titles, orders, styles and decorations that go to make up the British honours system settled officially into its present rigid and sacred pattern.

It is only necessary to consider the position of royalty themselves in the evolution of society, and the often quite arbitrary modes of address they have enjoyed, to realize that what we take for granted today is relatively recent in origin. It was not until the reign of James I that the title Majesty was used exclusively by the sovereign, Your Grace and Highness being common forms of address in the time of Henry VIII and Elizabeth I. And as a princess, Queen Elizabeth would never have been addressed as Royal Highness; most probably as Your Grace, Madam or the Lady Elizabeth.

While making allowances for the lack of a distinct time-scale by which to measure the creation of specific ranks in the peerage it is also necessary to appreciate the parallel and again haphazard development of perhaps the most crucial aspect of the honours system, knighthood — itself parcelled up into various orders, all of varying antiquity and seniority. Documentary evidence for the creation of the Order of the Garter and the Order of the Thistle is scant, to say the least, and these orders are of recent innovation compared to the basic concept of knighthood itself, from which they sprang. I have tried, I hope successfully, to separate the strands of the honours system in an intelligible way, but in so doing I am well aware that events inevitably overlap. Anyone who wishes to

Introduction

make a detailed — probably a lifetime's — study of the subject will find this book no more than a stepping-off point. Those who are content to accept the honours system as a part of history, to stand back and marvel at its foibles and chuckle at its absurdities (for surely, while occasionally marking both true merit and outstanding bravery, it does more frequently pander to the ridiculous side of our natures), and then to pass on to intellectual pursuits of a slightly more demanding nature, may be assisted if they bear in mind one or two salient points.

The British honours system contains three main components: the peerage, knighthood and decorations.

The peerage contains five basic grades: duke, marquess, earl, viscount and baron.

Knighthood consists of orders of chivalry, of which today there are six (the Garter, the Thistle, the Bath, St Michael & St George, the Royal Victorian and the British Empire), and knights bachelor.

Decorations range from the Victoria Cross to the British Empire Medal.

In addition to those orders of chivalry which involve knighthood, there are two important orders of chivalry which carry no title; the Order of Merit and the Companionship of Honour.

If this brief précis of honours is compared to the glossary appended it will be seen how scant an outline it represents, or conversely, how diversified, with knights grand cross and knights commanders, companions and members, the honours system is. Add to the basic list of peers those who hold courtesy titles, and consider the proper way to address the daughter of an earl should she marry beneath her, and it becomes all too easy to drown in a sea of snobbery and social gaffes. My advice to those already in the know is not to take the system or themselves too seriously, and to newcomers, just to hold on to the essentials, to take the temperature with one toe and then to enjoy a harmless bathe.

No one is responsible for any errors that follow except

myself, nor for any opinions expressed unless they are clearly quoted. I make this point specifically because a number of people closely involved with the distribution of honours have been kind enough to talk to me in relation to their job, not in any personal capacity.

Extracts from letters and diaries in the Royal Archives are reproduced by gracious permission of Her Majesty the Queen. A quotation from *Recollections of Three Reigns* by Sir Frederick Ponsonby appears by permission of Macmillan, and quotations from an article entitled "*Honi soit qui mal y pense*", which appeared in *The Times* on 25 May 1976, are the copyright of Mr Bernard Levin. In writing about the reigns of James I and Charles I, I have relied heavily upon Lawrence Stone's monumental work *The Crisis of the Aristocracy: 1558-1641*. Chapters concerned with the reign of George V owe more than they decently should to the painstaking research that went into Kenneth Rose's superb biography, *King George V*. And I need hardly say that I learned much from *Maundy Gregory: Purveyor of Honours* by Tom Cullen. A list of other books I have consulted will be found elsewhere. For information or assistance of one kind or another I am further indebted to Dr E. G. W. Bill (Librarian at Lambeth Palace), Mr Rodney Dennys (Arundel Herald of Arms), Sir Edward Ford (secretary to the Order of Merit), the Rt Hon Lord Franks, Mrs Ruth Gardner, Mrs Mary Hedley-Millar (the Ceremonial Officer), Mr Peter Hennessy, Mr Christopher Hibbert, Lt-Col Sir John Johnston (Comptroller in the Lord Chamberlain's Office), Mr Charles Kidd and Mr David Williamson of *Debrett's*, the Rt Hon Neil Kinnock, MP, Sir Robin Mackworth-Young (Librarian Emeritus to the Queen), Sir Michael Maxwell-Scott, Bt (secretary of the Standing Council of the Baronetage), Mr Austin Mitchell, MP, Miss Josephine Pullein-Thompson, Major-General Desmond Rice (secretary to the Central Chancery of the Orders of Knighthood), the Rt Hon Lord Shackleton (chairman of the Political Honours Scrutiny Committee), the Rt Hon David Steel, MP, His Grace the Duke of Wellington, the Rt Hon Lord

Introduction

Wilson of Rievaulx and the staff of *The Times* and the *Guardian* libraries.

MICHAEL DE-LA-NOY
London W2

The Principal British Honours

THE PEERAGE:
    Dukes
    Marquesses
    Earls
    Viscounts
    Barons

THE BARONETAGE: (James I, 1611)

DECORATIONS:
    The Victoria Cross (Queen Victoria, 1856)
    The George Cross (George VI, 1940)
    The Distinguished Service Order (Queen Victoria, 1886)

ORDERS OF CHIVALRY:
    The Most Noble Order of the Garter (Edward III, 1348)
    The Most Ancient and Most Noble Order of the Thistle (Revived by James II, 1687)
    The Most Honourable Order of the Bath (Revived by George I, 1725)
    The Order of Merit (Edward VII, 1902)
    The Most Distinguished Order of St Michael & St George (George IV, 1818)
    The Royal Victorian Order (Queen Victoria, 1896)
    The Royal Victorian Chain (Edward VII, 1902)
    The Most Excellent Order of the British Empire (George V, 1917)
    The Order of the Companions of Honour (George V, 1917)
    Knights Bachelor (circa 1220)

THE PRIVY COUNSELLORSHIP:

Glossary

The following abbreviations, commonly used as prefixes or as initials after people's names in the context of the honours system, are listed alphabetically, not in order of precedence. The list is not definitive; a number of orders carry no prefix, and a number of awards no medal or distinguishing initials.

Bart or Bt: denotes a baronetcy.
BEM: British Empire Medal.
CB: Companion of the Order of the Bath.
CBE: Companion of the Order of the British Empire.
CGM: Conspicuous Gallantry Medal (Navy and RAF).
CH: Companion of Honour.
CMG: Companion of the Order of St Michael & St George.
CVO: Companion of the Royal Victorian Order.
DBE: Dame Commander of the Order of the British Empire.
DCB: Dame Commander of the Order of the Bath.
DCM: Distinguished Conduct Medal (Army).
DCMG: Dame Commander of the Order of St Michael & St George.
DCVO: Dame Commander of the Royal Victorian Order.
DFC: Distinguished Flying Cross (RAF).
DFM: Distinguished Flying Medal (RAF).
DSC: Distinguished Service Cross (Navy).
DSM: Distinguished Service Medal (Navy).
DSO: Distinguished Service Order (all services).
GBE: Knight or Dame Grand Cross of the Order of the British Empire.

The Honours System

GC: George Cross.

GCB: Knight or Dame Grand Cross of the Order of the Bath.

GCMG: Knight or Dame Grand Cross of the Order of St Michael & St George.

GCVO: Knight or Dame Grand Cross of the Royal Victorian Order.

GM: George Medal.

The Hon: denotes the son or daughter or the daughter-in-law of a viscount or baron or the younger son or the wife of a younger son of an earl.

KBE: Knight Commander of the Order of the British Empire.

KCB: Knight Commander of the Order of the Bath.

KCMG: Knight Commander of the Order of St Michael & St George.

KCVO: Knight Commander of the Royal Victorian Order.

KG: Knight Companion of the Order of the Garter.

KT: Knight Companion of the Order of the Thistle.

LVO: Lieutenant of the Royal Victorian Order.

MBE: Member of the Order of the British Empire.

MC: Military Cross (Army).

MM: Military Medal (Army).

MVO: Member of the Royal Victorian Order.

OBE: Officer of the Order of the British Empire.

OM: Order of Merit.

The Right Hon: denotes a member of the Privy Council.

VC: Victoria Cross (all services).

CHAPTER ONE
"A Greate Heart's Ease"

The most immediately distinctive feature of a society dependent upon monarchy is the existence of titles of honour.
  Lawrence Stone, The Crisis of the Aristocracy.

The honours system is rooted not just in history but in the concept of the universe upon which Christian civilization came to base the very structure of society. That concept took the form of a pyramid, a permanent and stable edifice in which each brick — each person — had a well defined place and purpose, inter-dependent upon all the other bricks, starting with the king at the top and ending with the lowliest scurvy knave, or kitchen skivvy as the Victorian female equivalent became. The king took his orders from God and passed them down through a hierarchical army of law enforcers. Within this empire of worker ants were cells called families, all imitating the overall pattern of subservience to a father-figure, of obedience to rules regulating position and authority, privilege and prospects. The uncomplaining acceptance in Saxon, feudal and medieval times of gross inequality within every facet of society had its psychological origins in religious experience, in belief in the existence of a personal God as creator of heaven and earth and arbitrary distributor of favours in this world and the next, a belief shared by virtually every man and woman until at least the seventeenth century. The flames of this universal experience were fanned so furiously by the Church that through the one essential key to power, the possession of land, the clergy, not content with the cure of souls, came to share too in the governance of the people.

The point about the importance of land was made in 1669 when Edward Chamberlayne wrote: "The laws and customs of England . . . expected that each of [the degrees of honour] should have a convenient estate and value of lands of inheritance, for the support of their honours and the King's service." Due to poverty, between 1478 and 1523 the Duke of Bedford, the Marquess of Berkeley, Lord Clinton and the earls of Kent had failed to receive a summons to Parliament; and so strong was the necessary link felt to be between position and property that in 1629 the House of Lords petitioned Charles I to give the Earl of Oxford an estate so that he could support his dignity. Land provided income in the form of rents as well as retainers, and a penniless peer was not regarded as a pretty sight. To be fair to the prince-bishops and their desire to help rule the nation as well as the Church — in the north of England the bishops of Durham at one time held almost sovereign sway — they seemed to have sound scriptural authority in support of their secular ambitions. "Obey them that have the rule over you," they read in Hebrews 13:17, and in 1636 a member of the Goring family had the quotation inscribed on a wall of the church at Burton in Sussex, just in case his tenants should begin to feel any stirrings of social unrest. "Hold all innovations and new ways suspicious," admonished Sir Edward Coke, echoing the sentiments of every defender of the status quo through the ages, and it was, in large measure, for the purposes of maintaining the status quo that honours were invented. "A great temporall blessing it is, and a greate heart's ease to a man to find that he is well descended," sighed a sixteenth-century stalwart, Sir John Wynn, leaving it however to his contemporary Sir Simonds D'Ewes to explain how his and his companions' good fortune came about. "It [is]," Sir Simonds announced, "a great outward blessing to be well descended, it being in the gift only of God and nature to bestow it."

"A Greate Heart's Ease"

This dependence upon belief in direct benefit from on high was compounded by the traditional view of a sanctified social order, a society carved out to accommodate every individual according to the place chosen for him or her by God. "Though the magistrates be evil and very tyrants against the commonwealth and enemies to Christ's religion, yet the subjects must obey in all worldly things," Archbishop Cranmer informed those who had joined the peasants' revolt of 1549. It was sound theological teaching perfectly in tune with the aspirations of the Middle Ages.

Historians will argue, and often admit to considerable uncertainty, over the precise origins of historical development, and hardly surprisingly there lie buried in what romantic novelists like to call the mists of time many hazy and debatable starting points for the system of honours and rewards which has evolved into the present honours system. What is known for certain is that the general development of the honours system ran parallel with the development of monarchy, constitutional history and administration. At points where its origins and precise modes of development remain obscure, the same is usually true of many other customs and intentions of the times. But if hierarchy begat monarchy — the fountain of honour — it was military service which really gave birth to the honours system, for military service stood at the core of Western civilization, helping to lay down through the feudal structure a basis for the legal, political and social life that we enjoy — or revile — today. Military service gave rise to an establishment, and the honours system and the Establishment are inseparable.

While the peerage has come to rank in precedence above any order of knighthood, it is the concept and experience of knighthood which lies at the heart of the honours system, to the extent that knighthood itself came in time to be an honour conferred not just on professional soldiers but upon peers and kings themselves — as it still is today. Knighthood was introduced into England as early as the reign of Alfred the Great, king from 871-899, who knighted his own grandson, Athelstan. William II, for some reason not knighted by his father, was dubbed by Archbishop Lanfranc. Edward III was also knighted by a subject, as was the boy king Edward VI, by his uncle, the Duke of Somerset. James I gave the Garter to both his sons when they were 11, and Charles I, after losing his elder brother, went one better, bestowing the Garter on his own eldest son when the boy was 8. Charles had a dubious precedent to follow, for Henry VIII had made Henry Fitzroy, his illegitimate son, a Knight Companion of the Garter when he was only 7. Charles II was also later to pin the Garter to one of his illegitimate sons, Charles Lennox, shortly after the baby's birth.

So prized and glamorous at one time was the whole paraphernalia of knighthood that sovereigns sent their sons to foreign courts to be knighted at the hands of friendly kings. There was a religiosity and mysticism attached to knighthood. Knights were sworn to defend widows and orphans — many of whom were of their making. And this concept of a knight being available to fight in a good cause was to give a self-righteous impetus to the crusades. The lawlessness and physical hardships of the Middle Ages have now largely been diffused into the lush sentimentality of legend, but even if every knight was not Sir Galahad mooching around on a white charger, at least the concept of chivalry enshrined in knighthood gave a barbaric age some ideals worth aspiring to.

Knights, like barons and earls, came in time to play an integral part in the administration of the realm, the majority of administration in feudal times being synonymous with defence. In the reign of William I there were some five thousand knights prepared to fight under the command of the king's barons. Indeed, the creation and employment of knights had by then become a full-time occupation, and the barons, major landowners after the king and the Church, had authority to create knights themselves, who in turn received grants of land, farming out their land to sub-tenants, and retaining the right to call up these sub-tenants for military service. By the reign of Edward II, knighthood for those eligible had become almost compulsory, and any man holding

Crown land worth £20 a year had to accept knighthood or pay a fine.

No peerage has ever been created other than by the sovereign, but with the evolution of knighthood into almost a military rank, certainly a military command, consent for military commanders to dub in the name of the sovereign was sometimes granted. At the Battle of Wakefield in 1460 the Duke of Somerset and the Earl of Devonshire both dubbed four knights, and the Earl of Northumberland eight.

England's most ancient peerage is the earldom. Before Canute, who reigned from 1017-35, an earldorman was someone who administered a shire or province on behalf of the king. Earls in one guise or another are common to most European monarchies, and Canute, himself a Dane, introduced the Danish equivalent of an earl. Under the Normans an earldom was restricted to the governance of a county and became a hereditary post. A viscount (the word "count" is the European equivalent to an earl) was literally the deputy or lieutenant to a count or earl, from whose duties as an assistant in the governing of a county has derived our present Lord-Lieutenant. As a constituent of the peerage, viscountcies took a long time to become established. Henry VI raised Baron Beaumont to the rank of Viscount Beaumont in 1440, but for many years a viscountcy was thought little better than a barony and definitely inferior to an earldom, and failed to find popularity until the seventeenth century.

It was William I who introduced barons into England. They held their land directly from the king, rapidly superseding in influence any pre-Conquest earls, for by the thirteenth century it was the barons who were summoned to the king's council, or Parliament, although not in a hereditary capacity until the reign of Edward III. The first baron to be created by patent with remainder to his male heirs was John Beauchamp de Holt, raised to the peerage as Baron Kidderminster in 1387 by Richard II. In some ways he may be regarded as the immediate forerunner of our hereditary peerage, but many complications as to inheritance were to be invented. Creation by writ, for example, as opposed to patent ensured that the succession would fall into abeyance (not extinction) should a peer leave two or more daughters, remaining in abeyance until only one daughter, or the sole heir of one of the daughters, survived. Such a case is pending today. Lady Berners, who succeeded her eccentric cousin Lord Berners, the writer and composer, in 1950, has co-heiresses to her fifteenth-century title, her two daughters, the Hon. Mrs Kirkham and the Hon. Mrs Pollock.

A title may also fall into abeyance through uncertainty over the succession, and calling a title out of abeyance or having it recreated can be a lengthy, costly and frustrating procedure. For many years the Reverend J. P. Haldane-Stevenson, who lives in Melbourne, Australia, has been striving to establish his right to the barony of Eure, in abeyance since 1707, but despite petitioning in 1977 under the Bill of Rights and attempting to apply to Strasburg under article 6 of the European Convention on Human Rights he has so far failed to make any headway. A list of extinct, abeyant, dormant and suspended peerages, still reasonably up to date, was produced by L. G. Pine in *The New Extinct Peerage: 1884-1971*.[1]

The majority of peerages, however, only descend through the male line, usually from father to son, or in the event of a title already established in direct descent, to a brother, nephew or cousin; in the normal way, no first creation can be inherited other than by an eldest surviving son. But exceptions have been made to this general rule which underline as clearly as they possibly could one of the prime principles of a hereditary peerage: the perpetuation, come hell or high water, of an honoured and famous name. John Churchill, first Duke of Marlborough and certainly in his day the greatest soldier the country had yet produced, only had one surviving son, and when the young man died from smallpox at the age of 17, just a year after Churchill had received his dukedom, Parliament passed an Act permitting the duke's titles to descend through his daughters and their male heirs. Nelson had no legitimate children, and provision was made for the barony he had received after the Battle of the Nile (but not his later

1. Heraldry Today, 1972.

viscountcy) to be remaindered to his father and his father's sons, and, failing nephews, to nieces. In the event, Nelson was succeeded by his brother, but the government thought the hero of Trafalgar should be commemorated by something better than a barony, so the brother was created an earl.

Neither Field Marshal Kitchener nor Arthur Balfour were married, and both were created earls with special remainder to their brothers. Another Field Marshal, Allenby, victor of the Palestine Campaign against the Turks in the First World War, was created a viscount and was succeeded, by virtue of special remainder, by his nephew. Provision was made as recently as 1945 for Lord Portal of Hungerford and in 1947 for Earl Mountbatten of Burma for their new titles, bestowed in recognition of war service, to pass through the female line. But one of the most extraordinary series of provisions was reserved for a Viceroy of India, Lord Curzon, who had three daughters but no sons. When in 1911 he received an earldom, the courtesy viscountcy of Scarsdale was entailed to his father (and, in the event, it was inherited by Curzon's nephew) and the courtesy barony of Ravensdale was entailed through Curzon's daughters. His eldest daughter inherited, and by an unusual quirk of dynastic fate the title Lord Ravensdale descended to her nephew, the novelist Nicholas Mosley, who was also due to inherit a seventeenth-century baronetcy from the other side of his family, from his father, Sir Oswald Mosley.

Another weird and wonderful divergence from normal practice had been made by Charles I, who created Sir Baptist Hicks, a wealthy textile merchant, Viscount Campden, with remainder to his son-in-law. But odder by far was a pantomime performed in the twentieth century. Few will today recall the name or deeds of an oil magnate named Mr Urban H. Broughton, but so illustrious were they felt to be by a former generation that in 1929 the prime minister invited the king to make him a peer. Alas, before the letters patent could be granted Mr Broughton died. Nothing daunted, the government got the king to make his son a peer instead, and so came into existence Lord Fairhaven. But no one had foreseen the new noble lord's determination to remain a bachelor, and so worthy of perpetual remembrance was his father still felt to be that in 1961, when Lord Fairhaven was 65, yet another barony was conferred upon him (still in the name of Fairhaven), this time with special remainder to his brother, who succeeded in 1966. The nation has some cause to be grateful to the 1st Lord Fairhaven, however; like his father, he was extremely rich, and he made over his house, Anglesey Abbey near Cambridge, and the contents, to the National Trust. An amusing thumbnail sketch of Lord Fairhaven circa 1943 is to be found in *Ancestral Voices* by James Lees-Milne.[2]

Titles are currently held in their own right by five countesses and thirteen baronesses. The premier earldom of Scotland, which dates from 1115, is held by the Countess of Mar, and no less than nine of the baronesses' titles date from before the turn of the fifteenth century. Long before the 1958 Life Peerage Act, certain privileged ladies were actually created peeresses in their own right, as duchesses; these were some of the mistresses of Charles II, who between them bore him no fewer than thirteen illegitimate children.

Our senior peers, the dukes, have ridden some tumultuous times. The word duke derives from the Latin *dux*, a leader. Dukedoms have always been conferred sparingly, because kings themselves (William I is the best-known example) tended to hold dukedoms and were unattracted by the idea of their subjects enjoying rival status. Dukedoms have therefore most commonly been reserved for royalty, Edward III conferring the dukedom of Cornwall on his eldest son, the Black Prince, in 1337. The first non-royal dukedom did not come into existence until 1448, when William de la Pole, Marquess of Suffolk, was advanced to Duke of Suffolk. Elizabeth I felt able to get along without any dukes at all after her cousin Norfolk was executed for treason in 1572, and it was not until James I lost his head by making his ill-fated young lover, George Villiers, duke of Buckingham that the most senior rank in the peerage was resurrected.

The peer which ranks between a duke and an earl, the

2. London, Chatto and Windus, 1975.

marquess, can be traced back directly to the territorial traditions of Norman England, for a marchio was the earl or baron responsible for guarding the border lands, the Welsh or Scottish marches. By the twelfth century the title had lost touch with its original derivation, but something similar had evolved in Germany, where the count or *graf* had become a *markgraf*, anglicized to margrave. Richard II's brother-in-law was the Margrave of Brandenburg, and in 1385 the king introduced the title into England, anglicizing it still further by creating Robert de Vere, Earl of Oxford, marquess of Dublin.

The hierarchical administrative machinery of medieval England threw out so many tentacles that some form of status had to be found for almost everyone, and not content with knights and barons and earls, sheriffs and under-sheriffs, bailiffs and burghers, the ubiquitous esquire was invented. A knight himself was in one sense no more than someone who attended on a baron, and the knight needed someone to attend on him, and to learn the arts of chivalry and war, for apart from ordination there was virtually no other occupation open to a boy unless he was a labourer. The esquire — the word comes from *scutarius*, a shield bearer — was in effect an apprentice knight. It was not a title conferred, nor did it ever form any part of the hierarchy proper, and with the demise of the chivalrous aspect of knighthood the style "esquire" fell not so much into disuse as into the hands of those with no other title who thought that it sounded better than nothing. One such was Samuel Pepys. Appointed secretary to Lord Montagu in 1660, he received his first letter addressed to Samuel Pepys, Esq. "God knows I was not a little proud," he recalled. He was of course nothing more than a clerk in the Admiralty. Pedants today will claim that, among others, those entitled to be addressed as Esquire include sheriffs, justices of the peace, the eldest sons of knights, Royal Academicians, Queen's Counsel, Deputy Lieutenants, Commissioners of the Court of Bankruptcy, and, if anything more absurd can be imagined, officers above the rank of naval lieutenant, captain and flight-lieutenant. It seems, however, inadvisable to address a letter to Admiral of the Fleet Sir Algernon Harbottle Esq, and perhaps the less said in this supposedly egalitarian age on the subject of esquires the better.

So far as it can ever be compared with the rigmarole in existence today, the honours system in its origins was the product of an attempt to establish some sort of stable government and law-enforcement framework. In the most simplistic terms, knights fended off evil and fought for the king, barons helped the king to frame law and administer the country. The fact that from time to time many of them went about pillaging, raping, burning other people's homes and plotting against the king is another story. But by and large, knighthood before the Restoration went through transitional periods of being shrouded in chivalrous mystique, bestowed for valour, and being made practically compulsory, while the peerage evolved through co-operative but compulsory participation in government and then through a hereditary phase based partly on reward for services rendered, partly on a desire to create a ruling élite. Eventually the metamorphosis from autocracy to democracy, from absolutism to constitutional monarchy left the peerage in control of one-half of Parliament and the middle classes in receipt of nine-tenths of the honours.

Much of the ground-work for the eventual transition was laid in Tudor times, a period of astonishing commercial expansion and social mobility. The Tudor royal family were themselves little better than parvenus (after usurping the crown at the Battle of Bosworth, Henry VII had to get one of his new subjects to knight him), and a whole new industry began to thrive, the tracing of pedigree — not just back to the Norman Conquest but even to the Roman and Trojan Empires. Queen Elizabeth I's great servant Lord Burghley, newly ennobled of course, spent many happy hours browsing over spurious family trees. He was not alone among the new breed of insecure genealogists; in the next reign, Lord Lumley's foolish boast that he was related to the king drew from James I one of his many sardonic comments: "I did na ken Adam's name was Lumley."

Social climbing, snobbism and pretension, inevitable concomitants of any honours system, have flourished through the centuries. But the Tudors even went so far as to forge medieval seals and deeds, effigies and coats of arms, and the tracing of their ancestors became a national pastime. By 1577 the Earl of Essex had satisfied himself that he could legitimately lay claim to fifty-five quarterings, only to be outdone by the Grenville family, who collected a total of 719. Burghley decorated Theobalds with a map showing the coats of arms of every major landowner in the country, while his favoured contemporary, Elizabeth's Lord Chancellor, Sir Christopher Hatton, erected in the hall at Holdenby replicas of the arms of every peer in the land, together with all the gentry of his own county of Northamptonshire.

Every kind of attempt to buttress the hierarchical concept of society was made in Tudor and Elizabethan times. In 1591 Oxford University even allowed the sons of knights and peers to sit their Bachelor of Arts examination after three years instead of four, and by the reign of Charles I concern for rank and privilege had become so obsessive that in 1637 Thomas Bennett was fined £2,000 by the Star Chamber merely for claiming to be as good a gentleman as the Earl of Marlborough. Ludicrous though such a charge and penalty may seem to us today, no magisterial act of retribution on the part of the Establishment could better emphasize the whole purpose of the honours system as it had by then been practised for something like seven hundred years. If indeed a commoner was as good a gentleman as an earl, what was the point in being Earl of Marlborough? In its day it was a truly revolutionary claim. It was also no doubt intended by Mr Bennett as a sly dig at the dishonour into which the honours system had fallen, for by the reign of Charles I the sale of peerages and baronetcies and the wholesale knighting of worthy nobodies had reached epidemic proportions.

The hallmark of a gentleman in Mr Bennett's day was that he had no occupation by which he earned a living. Like Oscar Wilde's Lady Harbury in *The Importance of Being Earnest* 258 years later, he lived entirely for pleasure, the aesthetic pursuit of which was considered an end in itself, and upon which he spent, and sometimes ostentatiously squandered, a private income almost always derived from land, for trade and commerce conducted in the city were not considered respectable. Certain social obligations fell upon a gentleman, however: to dress well, to cultivate decent table manners and to entertain. The disadvantage of being merely a gentleman — someone without a profession and probably without access to court — was lack of any reward or, as we would say today, job satisfaction. It may have occurred to Mr Bennett, as it certainly did to others of his class, that being a gentleman was all very well but being a lord was better, for advancement to the peerage was the only ambition open to a gentleman, and in Mr Bennett's time, social mobility was as rampant as the sale of peerages was rife. It may be that a touch of sour grapes had added zest to his indiscretions.

The gentry had been aspiring to the peerage for the past two hundred years. Members of the College of Heralds had made fat fortunes out of inventing pedigrees for the *nouveaux riches*, a scandal that came to a head in 1579 when in Cheshire a herald of dubious credentials was discovered to have tricked nearly ninety of the gentry into accepting entirely fictitious family trees and coats of arms. Land had changed hands in Elizabeth's reign so rapidly that 4,000 grants of arms were made between 1560 and the eve of the Civil War. In 1433 a county like Shropshire contained only 48 families claiming the status of gentry; by the Restoration, Yorkshire, for example, was inhabited by 700. Part of this social upsurge, which was eventually to bring the honours system into such disrepute, with newly risen gentlemen anxious to go a step further up the ladder by paying for a peerage, was marked by the right of heralds to sell their wares, a right that inevitably led to bribery and corruption. In 1639 both the resplendently named Norroy King of Arms and the Somerset Herald were sacked for forgery, but by that time discipline within the College of Heralds had become chaotic; in 1616, Garter King of Arms, Sir William Segar, had been tricked by the York Herald into selling a coat of arms for 22 shillings to the London hangman, and both heralds were sent to prison by James I for

"A Greate Heart's Ease"

lèse-majesté when he discovered that the arms in question belonged to the House of Aragon.

James had better reason perhaps than many sovereigns to feel his proprietorial feathers ruffled by such presumption. He recognized the value of honours in more ways than one, and while it may be thought that the honours system has been brought into greater disrepute during other reigns, it has never been more abused by any other monarch. This partly had to do with James's immature need to purchase affection (few men have ever ascended a throne from a more emotionally deprived background), and partly with the historical development of the distribution of honours. In the reign of Henry VI the number of knights was estimated, by 1439, to have fallen to 250. Edward IV and his sons increased their numbers slightly, but it was under Henry VII and his son and grandchildren that the wealthy Tudor families, eager to establish social respectability by discovering an impressive pedigree, desired and were often granted a title to embellish their newly acquired lands and prestige. From the middle of Henry VIII's reign until the death of Mary I, the Tudors created about seventeen knights a year, so that when Elizabeth I came to the throne there were something like six hundred. She failed, however, to continue creating new knights at a sufficient rate either to replace those who died or to begin to satisfy the craving for glory that marked her age, and the numbers (but not the quality) were only kept topped up at all by the sometimes reckless distribution of honours on the Queen's behalf, by the Earl of Essex — who shot his bolt by knighting 81 of his own followers in Ireland in 1599 — and by Lord Howard of Effingham, who brought his Cadiz expedition of 1596 into ridicule by dubbing sixty-eight new knights, many of whom had only gone abroad to gain a knighthood in the first place. Those of Elizabeth's subjects who had advanced their own standing in the shires, who had built and entertained on a massive scale, had helped to administer justice and to distribute charity to the poor, and had even stooped to engage in commerce to the benefit of the nation's purse as well as their own, felt deprived of proper recognition and thanks. By the time Elizabeth's languid cousin had come lisping south to claim his inheritance the English bourgeoisie had outgrown Elizabethanism, was poised at the start of a new century, and was anxious to share in the spoils of an easy-going and generous benefactor desperate for friends, affection and money. Elizabeth had never travelled further north than Leicester, so that for all her boasts to have united her kingdom, the majority of her subjects had never set eyes on her, and the new king's journey south, irrespective of the largesse in store, had the effect of opening up the person of the monarch in an entirely new way.

James VI of Scotland inherited the throne of England on 24 March 1603. Within four months he had created 906 new knights. One morning, while staying at Belvoir on his way to London, he dubbed forty-six knights before breakfast. He had never set foot in England before, he had scarcely been kept informed of English life and customs, and before long men were queuing up to offer bribes to his Scottish courtiers to be recommended for a title. There was no way for the king to sift the applicants. He came from a comparatively impoverished land, and so ignorant was he of English economics that he ordered anyone worth £40 a year to present themselves for knighthood. Sir Thomas Tresham, who at least knew the financial situation of his own county, reckoned 400 men worth £40 a year could be found in Northamptonshire alone. London pedlars and heaven knows who else were soon strutting around as knights, and the playwrights had a field-day mocking the debasement of honour by creating such satirical characters as Sir Petronel Flash. The deluge of honours seemed unstoppable. On Coronation Day, 23 July 1603, 432 new knights were created in a single session. Francis Bacon considered knighthood now "almost prostituted" and promptly accepted the accolade. By March the following year £100 was the price being asked to have one's name recommended at court. Soon the king saw no reason why his courtiers should profit if he did not, so he began to sell the franchise, and by 1606 we find the right to nominate six

"A Greate Heart's Ease"

knights passing from Arthur Ingram to Lionel Cranfield for £373 1s 8d. But by that time, irresponsibility had run riot, the king having decided to knight his goldsmith for making a hole in one of his diamonds.

Instead of remaining as the fountain of honour, James I became the centre of an honours racket. Between 1605 and 1609 an average of 74 knighthoods were sold annually, which may not sound excessive but was in reality a carefully arrived at figure, just about the number that the market would bear if the price was not to fall. The king received £60 for each ceremony, and almost everyone took a rake-off, with sums payable to heralds and sergeants-at-arms and even to the king's jester. One herald claimed to hold himself above the fray, writing in 1604, "Without all doubt he that buyeth his knighthood loseth the honour of knighthood," and within seven years James himself had come to accept and apologize for the dishonour he had heaped upon the honours system. "Ye saw I made Knights then by hundreths and Barons in great numbers," he told Parliament on 21 March 1610, referring to his progress from Scotland to London, adding, "but I hope you find I doe not so now, nor mind to do so hereafter." But James was no more capable of relinquishing his love of patronage nor meeting his need for funds through the sale of favours than he was of ceasing to fawn on the necks of beautiful boys or eating and drinking until he was sick.

In 1547 there had been seventy-four peers. By 1625 there were 123, James I having conferred 108 English peerages on sixty-eight individuals, of whom twelve were already peers, while restoring five peerages and confirming the disputed title of a peeress. One of James's new earls was actually a pirate, and the king's affection for the noble seafarer's son may have accounted for this particular quirk. In 1618 the Bishop of Winchester told his brother, Sir Edward Montague: "If you have £10,000 in your purse, I think, if you know not how to bestow it better, you may have a barony for it." Three years later, he did. Financial transactions sometimes became incredibly complicated where the purchase of a peerage was concerned. Sir Thomas Finch's wealthy wife took a fancy to

The Honours System

become a countess in her own right, but after five years of protracted negotiations, involving the Duchess of Lennox and the Lord Treasurer, she settled for the viscountcy of Maidstone in exchange for her house, Copt Hall in Essex, a set of tapestries and £7,000. Thus today the schoolboy son of the Earl of Winchilsea & Nottingham (Christopher Finch-Hatton; in 1628 Lady Maidstone achieved her first ambition, and became a countess) enjoys the style and dignity of Viscount Maidstone.

In a reign lasting twenty-two years James I made 2,600 knights, and three years after the king's death the Venetian ambassador was reporting home, "the number of counsellors and titled persons . . . [is] so constantly multiplied that they are no longer distinguishable from common people." George Villiers, after Edward II's lover Piers Graveston perhaps the most famous and certainly the most notorious male favourite in England's history, gained not only a dukedom — Buckingham — for himself at the hands of James I, but for his family and friends and their relations so many dubious, debased and purchased honours that he was eventually bundled off the stage by a hired assassin, though not before he had faced impeachment for pocketing £10,000 when in 1625 Sir Richard Robartes achieved his life-long ambition of becoming Lord Robartes of Truro. By 1620 Villiers had been selling knighthoods at £100 a time — and to all and sundry; those who had received an honour once conferred for valour included the husband of the Queen's laundress, an innkeeper in Romford and the Earl of Montgomery's barber. Buckingham's murder, on 23 August 1628, was such a shock to Charles I, who loved him almost as much as his father had done, that the new king reacted by forbidding the sale of any more honours, a decision bound to make him enemies, if only because he had had the nerve three years before to threaten to fine anyone who refused to take up knighthood at his coronation. By this means, in five years he raised £173,537.

The barter of peerages between 1615-28 resulted in some £200,000 changing hands. Sir John Roper purchased his barony for £10,000 in 1616, but had the misfortune to die two

"A Greate Heart's Ease"

years later at the age of 83. £10,000 was also the sum paid for their peerages by Lord Dormer, in 1615, and Lord Haughton, in 1616. It appears to have been the going rate for a barony. Eight years later Haughton was advanced to an earldom on payment of a further £5,000. Despite his own blatant behaviour he had the cheek to object, unsuccessfully, to an earldom for his wife's kinsman, Sir Philip Stanhope, on the grounds that Sir Philip had twice been up before the Star Chamber accused of sodomy. Roper himself had for many years run a lucrative sinecure called the Clerkship of Enrolments in the King's Bench, an office at that time in the gift of the Lord Chief Justice. After Roper's death this sinecure fell into the hands of George Villiers, and through its machinations he sold at least nine peerages. Other peers and peeresses were equally tainted by the sale of honours, among them the Earls of Carlisle, Arundel, Pembroke, March, Oxford and Mulgrave, Viscount Conway and the Duchess of Richmond. Between 1603-29 something like £650,000 was raised by the sale of peerages alone, over £100,000 being creamed off by the broker peers before James and Charles got their share. In his invaluable study of Elizabethan and Stuart England, *The Crisis of the Aristocracy, 1558-1641*, Lawrence Stone has written, "Unattractive though it may be to those with romantic illusions about rank and title, it has been the successful fusion of old blood, new wealth and political careerism that has given the English peerage its remarkable capacity for survival over the past three centuries." Yet had the Commonwealth not intervened, to be followed by Charles II, a sovereign with an astute instinct for survival, with sound common sense and a sense of the dignity of his office and the state, by the end of the seventeenth century the entire honours system, through ridicule and contempt, might well have ground to an ignominious halt.[3]

---

3. As republics go, the Commonwealth was nevertheless a lukewarm affair, as reluctant to abolish hereditary titles as it had been to execute the king; Cromwell actually created five baronets, although the absolute legality of their creation may be doubted by constitutional lawyers.

CHAPTER TWO
Lords and Ladies

As regards [Lord Alfred Douglas] . . . I have written to him to tell him that . . . for him to try and pose as your social superior because he is the third son of a Scotch marquis and you the third son of a commoner is offensively stupid. There is no difference between gentlemen. Questions of title are matters of heraldry — no more.

Oscar Wilde in a letter to Robert Ross.

Few countries muddle along without an honours system of some sort, for it is quite simply the cheapest method of rewarding and encouraging those the state holds in esteem or to whom it may even consider it owes its survival. John Churchill received Blenheim Palace as well as the dukedom of Marlborough, and Haig £100,000 as well as an earldom, but with the advent of state pensions for all, financial gifts for the newly ennobled have rather gone out of fashion. Generally speaking, the modern plan as practised across a wide spectrum of ideologies is to enhance the prestige of those in authority, to recognize personal valour, to acknowledge outstanding artists and scientists, and to encourage contributors to the export and population drives.

It has sometimes got a little out of hand. According to Sir Frederick Ponsonby, assistant private secretary to Edward VII, at the turn of the century the Germans distributed 30,000 orders and decorations every year compared to England's 800, and on state visits the Emperor was quite likely to bestow between 300 and 500 decorations whereas the king restricted his to around 30.[1] But since the demise of post-First World War Ruritania, most countries (with the rather comical exception of Communist Russia) have restricted their list of honours to a handful of decorations and orders. And by and large these are distributed on the grounds of merit, not by virtue of any post the recipient may hold, or to match his or her class or social status. Usually, too, they carry no embellishment of any specific title. The peerage itself has throughout history been confined almost exclusively to European and Asian monarchies (African kings seem to have ruled perfectly satisfactorily without creating earls and viscounts, margraves and barons), and with only seven monarchies remaining in Western Europe today, the creation of new peers on the continent is practically unheard of.[2] Pretenders, like the Comte de Paris, are not averse to bestowing dukedoms on their offspring, but such a practice is generally regarded with the sly tolerance traditionally reserved for personable eccentrics.

Britain, on the other hand, is a little different. In the course of approximately one thousand years it has developed the most complex, class-ridden and — to all but a handful of civil servants, courtiers and snobs — the most baffling honours system in the world, and for foreigners it is a perpetual nightmare. In 1984, Christie's in Rome catalogued a sale of autographs, attributing them to Lady Margaret Thatcher, Sir Anthony Wedgwood Benn and Sir Kenneth Livingstone, seemingly on the principle that if someone is famous it is reasonable to assume they must have a title. On 24 June 1981, in a televised attack on the British government, the Israeli prime minister Mr Begin referred to the Foreign Secretary and the Lord Privy Seal as Mr Carrington and Mr Gilmour. Yet who can blame him when even *The Times* allows solecisms to

1. *Recollections of Three Reigns* (London, Eyre and Spottiswoode, 1951).
2. Belgium, Denmark, the Netherlands, Norway, Spain, Sweden and the United Kingdom. Liechtenstein and Monaco are principalities, Luxemburg is a grand duchy and the Vatican City is ruled by a sovereign pontiff.

slip past sub-editors and proof-readers with gay abandon; on 15 October 1984 they twice referred to Lady Alexandra Metcalfe, the daughter of a marquess, as Lady Metcalfe, and in the same article referred to her sister, Lady Cynthia Mosley, as Lady Mosley. On 18 November 1984 the *Sunday Times* even called Viscountess Long "Viscountess Margaret Long", having the week before described Lady Traill, wife of the Lord Mayor of London, as Lady Sarah Traill.

The British honours system has survived a civil war and a revolution led by royalty themselves, two world wars and two decades of socialist government. Its complexity is such that it provides sources of information and areas of research for the historical novelist, the student of social history and the aspiring politician; it provides a full-time living for men and women who keep its records up-to-date and administer its development; it perpetuates myths about inherited ability, enables the state to regulate patterns of excellence, and twice a year feeds into the hearts of thousands of ordinary men, women and children perfectly ordinary human emotions, like envy, bitterness, pride and pleasure.

The honours system contains two prime components: a graded selection of orders, mainly of chivalry, together with decorations for gallantry; and the peerage. If it is true — and it very probably is not — that the only advantage in being a peer today is that you need not sit on a jury and that it helps you to reserve the best table in a restaurant, the privileges enjoyed by peers in the past raised their enjoyment of life, not to mention their life expectancy, well above that of the common man. They could only be arrested for treason, felony or causing a breach of the peace, they were not obliged to testify under oath (this perhaps is the origin of the saying "a gentleman's word is his bond"), their income tax was assessed by commissioners answerable to their fellow peers, and they could expect almost automatically to fill many of the high offices of state. During the reign of Charles I, twenty-nine out of thirty-three Lord-Lieutenants were noblemen; in 1983 only eleven out of forty-six were peers. In Tudor times, peers could cast their votes in the House of Lords by proxy, so that they scarcely even needed to travel to Westminster to legislate for the nation. Today a peer must attend to vote, but he has quite a pleasant inducement to do so, an attendance allowance of £36 a day plus secretarial expenses, free access to car parking and most of the facilities of a very comfortable club, including an inexhaustible supply of writing paper. In order to collect his allowance he need only sign in, not out, for in best public-school tradition he is placed only under a moral obligation to remain on the premises for any reasonable length of time.

More to the point, the British peerage remains unique, in a democracy, in providing an unelected and partially self-perpetuating second chamber in Parliament. And because the British are partial both to democracy and to privilege, they tend to hold even a life peer in greater awe than a Knight Companion of the Most Noble Order of the Garter. Some of those who receive honours, however, entertain a more balanced set of values. A man of letters, with no ambition to debate the Urban Parishes Bill, would probably treasure as an appropriate estimate of the true value of his achievements appointment to the Companionship of Honour rather than a peerage or even the Garter, whereas a civil servant, obviously without political aspirations, will be looking for automatic promotions within the Most Distinguished Order of St Michael & St George with which to celebrate his equally automatic progress up the career ladder.

No matter what view one may hold of the desirability of a seat in the House of Lords as opposed to wearing round one's neck the carmine ribbon of the CH, beneath the monarchy the peerage forms the apex of the pyramid of precedence. Everyone loves a lord, and a great many people over the centuries have wanted to be one. To a large extent the peerage is inherently a constituent part of Parliament, and hence of the governance of the realm, and in spite of the 1958 Life Peerage Act it is impossible not to consider the hereditary principle as still a vital component of the honours system. For one thing, the 1958 Act did not abolish the hereditary element within the House of Lords, nor in the country at large, inhabited as it is by cohorts of assorted aristocracy who enjoy styles and titles which in turn earn them unearned status and privilege. And since the passing of the Act, no fewer than forty-one hereditary peers (two earls, ten viscounts and twenty-nine barons) have been created.[3] With certain exceptions, any hereditary peer of the realm may take his seat in the House of Lords (and since the 1963 Peerage Act, any hereditary peeress in her own right). Scottish peers elect sixteen of their number to sit in the House of Lords, while the remainder are debarred from both the House of Lords and the House of Commons; Irish peers may not sit in the House of Lords but they can stand for a non-Irish constituency. In spite of threats to abolish the hereditary principle in Parliament made before all-party talks on reform of the House of Lords were broken off by Harold Wilson in 1968, the hereditary element in Parliament and the country remains alive and well, encouraging and contributing to the "grading system" reflected within the most widely distributed orders of knighthood, and even within the distribution of decorations for gallantry.

Within the peerage there are peers and peers of the realm. Peers of the realm are peers or peeresses with titles in their own right who are eligible to sit in the House of Lords. This they may do at the age of 21, so long as they are both solvent and sane. If peers wish to sit in the House of Commons they must disclaim their peerage for life. Oddly enough, a shocking criminal record is no bar to membership of a club still regarded by many as the most exclusive in London; Lord Spens, an accountant and a Queen's Counsel, sat on the cross benches until his death on 23 November 1984, having been sent to prison for two and a half years in 1974 for stealing £151,000 from the Federation of British Carpet Manufacturers, a sum he had then proceeded to lose by gambling.

A peer of the realm will hold at least one of five titles, duke, marquess, earl, viscount or baron, and unless he is a duke he is customarily addressed as "Lord Northampton" (or whatever name is appropriate). A duke is styled "Your Grace" by servants and those who are prepared to run the risk of being

---

3. These figures, and similar statistics, were accurate at the time of writing.

thought lower middle class; his social equals call him "Duke" or "Sir". Almost invariably, every duke, marquess and earl holds one or more junior titles (which may have been bestowed on descendants on the way up or may all have been bestowed on a first creation, although very few people other than prime ministers and war leaders have ever received an honour higher than a viscountcy on first being raised to the peerage); these are known as courtesy titles, the most senior of which is adopted by the eldest son, providing it does not clash with the primary title. Earl Mountbatten of Burma, for example, was also Viscount Mountbatten of Burma, so that the present Countess Mountbatten's eldest son uses his late grandfather's barony of Romsey. In England, no heir presumptive takes a courtesy title, although in Scotland the heir presumptive to a baron is styled "The Master of Gray" (for example) until the birth of an heir apparent. No female heir presumptive even to a title remaindered through the female line may use a courtesy title, for fear she does not in the end succeed. These English eldest sons, peers who hold courtesy titles (the Duke of Abercorn's heir, for example, is the 15-year-old Marquess of Hamilton, one of the pages of honour who carried the Queen's train at the state opening of Parliament on 6 November 1984), are eligible to sit in the House of Commons, so strictly speaking they are also commoners. The younger sons of dukes and marquesses take courtesy titles in the style "Lord John Manners", and they too are politely regarded as peers, in so far as the butler will address them as "My Lord"; their social equals call them "Lord John" and their wives "Lady John"; anyone who addresses the spouse of a younger son as "Lady Manners" seldom gets invited to dinner twice. The daughters of a duke, a marquess or an earl are correctly styled as "Lady Jane Manners", and retain their title of Lady Jane when they marry, adopting their husband's surname, unless they marry higher in the order of precedence. Likewise the daughters of a viscount or baron retain their own right to the prefix The Hon., although they would drop the prefix if they married a peer.

There is one exception to the rules governing courtesy titles.

In 1917, King George V decided by letters patent that all grandchildren of the sons of the sovereign in the direct male line should have the style and dignity enjoyed by the children of dukes. Hence the children of Prince Michael of Kent, although he is not a duke, are known as Lord Frederick Windsor and Lady Ella Windsor, whereas the children of his sister, Princess Alexandra, their father being a commoner (the Hon. Angus Ogilvy, a son of the 12th Earl of Airlie), have no titles at all. The children of Princess Anne and Captain Mark Phillips are in the same position as those of Princess Alexandra. It was suddenly realized in 1948, when Princess Elizabeth was expecting her first child, that any children of her marriage to the Duke of Edinburgh would derive their status not from their mother but their father, and on 9 November 1948 it was thought necessary for King George VI by letters patent to declare that any children of Princess Elizabeth should hold and enjoy the style, title or attribute of Royal Highness and the titular dignity of a prince or princess. Had this not been done, Prince Charles would have been born Earl of Merioneth and his sister and brothers would be Lady Anne, Lord Andrew and Lord Edward Mountbatten. But no similar provision was made for any possible children born to Princess Margaret; closer to the throne than Prince Michael's by a generation, her children, like Princess Anne's, would have been without titles of any sort had not their father, Anthony Armstrong-Jones, been created Earl of Snowdon after his marriage. These are anomalies which could be put right at any time, and presumably they originally arose because in 1917 — no daughter of a sovereign having married a commoner since Princess Cicely, daughter of Edward IV, married Thomas Kymbe in 1503 — George V did not envisage the daughters of the sovereign marrying commoners, and certainly not their husbands remaining commoners. Presumably also part of the argument for not extending the letters patent of 14 December 1917 to include children in the female line is that should their mother marry a commoner they would hold a title while their father, unless later ennobled, would not.

There are of course no limits to the rules of precedence and etiquette that the sovereign may invent or sanction. There seems, for example, no clear rule for the nomenclature of commoners who marry a prince. The Princess of Wales (who is improperly referred to as Princess Diana, although one day, presumably, she will be Queen Diana) and Princess Michael of Kent have both adopted their husband's titles, as they would had they married a peer, and in the past, a princess in her own right, like Queen Victoria's youngest daughter, Princess Beatrice, has also usually adopted her husband's title (she became known as Princess Henry of Battenberg). Yet when the Duke of Gloucester's father died his mother, who is not a princess in her own right, decided to style herself Princess Alice, not Princess Henry. The oddest aberration by far is the addiction of Princess Anne and Princess Alexandra to tagging the prefix Mrs on to their own name in the Court Circular when both are the daughters of dukes.

Sometimes it is difficult to tell whether royal anomalies are deliberate or the result of an oversight. On the eve of Lieutenant Philip Mountbatten's wedding, King George VI invested him with the Garter, and the next day created him Baron Greenwich, Earl of Merioneth and Duke of Edinburgh, at the same time granting him the style His Royal Highness. In doing so, however, the king, whether intentionally or not, had failed to ensure that his son-in-law became a prince (he had renounced his Greek title), and for a decade he was often incorrectly referred to as Prince Philip; it was not until 1957 that the Queen regulated the matter by granting the Duke of Edinburgh the style and titular dignity of Prince of the United Kingdom. An earlier aberration on the part of King George VI had occurred in 1936 when, faced with no precedent, he reinstituted the former Edward VIII as a Royal Highness after his abdication but compelled the new Duke of Windsor to undergo a morganatic marriage by deliberately withholding from the Duchess the title Royal Highness. It was a particularly cruel blow as the former king, while negotiating his constitutional and emotional problems before abdication, had asked for a morganatic marriage as king and had been refused one. It was doubted by many at the time, and is doubted by many more today, whether George VI actually had it in his power to withhold from the wife of a prince the rank of a princess. It had never been done before, and in view of the legacy of unease it has left it is unlikely, given even remotely similar circumstances, to be an error of judgement committed again.

The English duke in literature is frequently portrayed as eccentric and a figure of fun, immensely rich with a wife bedraggled with diamonds, the port-besotted inhabitant of a creaking castle surrounded by a moat, waited upon twenty-four hours a day by loyal and aged retainers and guarded from the proles by a pack of frenzied bloodhounds. Some dukes are like this, but in reality their one common denominator is the selectively of their numbers — a mere twenty-six, excluding the royal dukes. Three of them share the spoils of socially acceptable illegitimacy and an equal quantity of Charles II's blood. As a reminder of his distinguished ancestry, the Duke of Grafton, a friend as well as a distant cousin of the Queen (his wife is Mistress of the Robes), was actually christened FitzRoy. The mother of the first Duke of Grafton, Lady Castlemaine, who bore Charles at least five children, was created Duchess of Cleveland for life. Charles Beauclerk, the son of Charles and Nell Gwynn, was created Duke of St Albans when he was fourteen, and Charles Lennox, the son of Louise Renée de Penancoet de Keroualle (whom Charles made Duchess of Portsmouth for life), became Duke of Richmond at the age of three. His present descendants, the Duke of Richmond & Gordon and his son, the Earl of March & Kinrara, annually entertain the Queen for Goodwood Races.

Dukedoms, especially royal dukedoms, have come and gone with dazzling rapidity. Only one surviving dukedom, Norfolk, retains links with the Middle Ages, and only one other, Somerset, with Tudor England. As many as nineteen trace their origins only to the seventeenth or eighteenth centuries, while by comparison with the most ancient earldoms and baronies, two, Abercorn (created in 1868) and Westminster (1874), seem positively parvenu. Another nineteenth-century creation, that of Wellington, was received with almost studied nonchalance. Writing in 1814 on Spanish affairs to his youngest brother, Sir Henry Wellesley, the victor of Vitoria remembered to add at the end of his letter: "I believe I forgot to tell you that I was made a Duke." No dukedom has been conferred, other than on royalty, since that of Fife in 1889. As Earl of Fife, the duke had married Edward VII's eldest daughter, Princess Louise, later the Princess Royal, but an earldom then was not considered good enough for the husband of a princess. (This dukedom was created with special remainder, in default of male heirs, to the duke's daughters, and in 1905 Edward conferred upon Princess Louise's daughters the very un-English title Highness.) When George V's daughter, Princess Mary, married Viscount Lascelles, heir to the Earl of Harewood (after he had been refused by Vita Sackville-West; no wonder he was known as Lucky Lascelles), Lord Harewood declined a marquessate, apparently on the superstitious grounds that marquesses died out more quickly than earls. By the time the new Princess Royal's niece, Princess Margaret, married a commoner, an earldom for her husband was considered adequate, and when her niece, Princess Anne, married a commoner too, no peerage of any sort was forthcoming, or probably desired. The last commoner to be offered a dukedom, by the Queen on her own initiative, was Sir Winston Churchill, on relinquishing leadership of the Tory Party, and he declined the honour. According to E. T. Williams's entry on Churchill in the *National Dictionary of Biography,* Churchill toyed in 1955 with the Dukedom of London (favoured in 1892 by Queen Victoria for the future George V), but rejected all ideas of a peerage because his son did not wish to go eventually to the House of Lords; it was not until the 1963 Peerage Act that a peer might disclaim his title for life.

There is no heir to the Duke of Portland, nor, at the time of writing, to the young Duke of Westminster. It is almost inconceivable that a dukedom will ever again be conferred other than on a prince consort, or a younger son of the sovereign, all of whom have received dukedoms since 1337 — the sons of Edward VII, however, being raised, or as Queen

Victoria thought, demoted, to the peerage by their grandmother most reluctantly. In 1890 the dozey Prince Albert was created Duke of Clarence & Avondale. "I am very sorry Eddy should be lowered to a Duke like any one of the nobility which a Prince can never be," Queen Victoria wrote. "Nothing is so fine and grand as a Royal Prince — but it is very good he should be a Peer." Referring to Eddy's younger brother, Prince George, she went on, "I don't think Georgie will ever be made a Duke in my lifetime." Two years later, Eddy was dead, and somewhat reluctantly the queen agreed to the prince now second in line to the throne taking the title Duke of York. "A Prince *no one* else can be," she still found the energy to declare, "whereas a Duke any nobleman can be, and many are!"

Queen Victoria's dislike of dukedoms for princes may have been a view, like so many of her attitudes, picked up from the Prince Consort, who wrote at the time of his engagement, when there was talk of granting him an English peerage, "It would be almost a step downwards, for as a Duke of Saxony I feel myself much higher than as Duke of Kent or York." Whatever the numerical strength of the dukes may have been in Queen Victoria's time, the fact is that today they are virtually doomed to extinction, unless from time to time their numbers are supplemented by the non-royal descendants of royal dukes, such as the Earl of Ulster, son of the Duke of Gloucester, and his successors, the Earl of St Andrews, son of the Duke of Kent, and his successors, and eventually the heirs to Prince Andrew and Prince Edward and of any younger sons who may be born to the Princess of Wales. But however uncertain their tenure, the wealth of the dukes remains, and seems likely to remain, prodigious. The first wife of the 1st Duke of Westminster, herself a daughter of the Duke of Somerset, attended the wedding of the then Prince of Wales and Princess Alexandra dripping in half a million pounds worth of jewels. The 2nd Duke of Westminster, who died in 1953, possessed two yachts, three houses in Scotland, one in London, two in France and one in Venice besides Eaton Hall in Cheshire, which alone could house 100 guests with a servant each. The present Duke's fortune, based on real estate, remains, on a day-to-day basis, quite simply impossible to calculate. When the 10th Duke of Beaufort died in 1984 he left £5,062,062. The same year, the Duke of Devonshire only had to auction seventy-one drawings to realize £21,179,880, thus ensuring for himself, after tax, an additional annual income of at least £1 million.

Marquesses are not much less select in number than dukes; there are at present only thirty-six, of whom two, Dufferin & Ava and Ormonde, have no heir. No marquess has been created since, in 1917, Prince Louis of Battenberg, who had married a granddaughter of Queen Victoria, was persuaded to renounce his German title in exchange for the marquessate of Milford Haven. Lord Downshire's parents did their best to keep his family's name in trim. To his nearest and dearest the present marquess is known as Arthur Wills Percy Wellington Blundell Trumbell Sandys Hill. But, like their cousins the dukes, the marquesses can only, in the natural order of things, be on the decline.

With the elevation of Mr Harold Macmillan as Earl of Stockton in 1984, the first earl to be created for twenty-three years, new heart will have been put into admirals, prime ministers and brewers, the kind of people who in more recent times have traditionally been honoured by an award that used to go to landowners, and who may hope for such an honour once again to fall into their lap. Mr Macmillan joined the ranks of some 200 earls, creations that span the years 1398 (Crawford) to 1961 (Avon and Snowdon). The younger sons of earls are styled "The Hon. John Smith" and referred to as "Mr Smith" (to introduce such a gentleman by his prefix is the ultimate social gaffe), but for reasons totally unconnected with logic, the daughters of an earl are called "Lady Jane Smith" and are addressed as "Lady Jane", the only instance within the entire honours system where it is possible to detect favouritism towards women. Even the right of a woman to succeed to the throne is dependent upon her having no brothers or any direct descendant, male or female, of her brothers.

Through another inexplicable quirk of social history, no viscount is ever accorded a courtesy title, so that all the

Lords and Ladies

children of viscounts and barons are styled "The Hon. John Smith" or "The Hon. Jane Smith". There are currently rather fewer viscounts than earls. Lords Eccles, Muirshiel and Watkinson, the last two without heirs, were the last viscounts to be created following the 1958 Life Peerage Act until Mrs Margaret Thatcher resurrected the creation of hereditary peerages in her 1983 Dissolution Honours List, when two politicians, again both without heirs, Mr William Whitelaw and Mr George Thomas, became Lord Whitelaw and Lord Tonypandy. At the other end of the timescale, the premier viscount of Ireland, Lord Gormanston, can trace his lineage back to 1478.

Barons, like earls, are endemic to the European peerage, and around 500 grace the pages of *Debrett's*. The most senior baron of England is Lord Mowbray, Segrave & Stourton, whose claim to the premier barony rests on his titles of Mowbray and Segrave, both created in 1283. When Lord Home became prime minister in 1963, Harold Wilson had fun sneering at his ancestry, on the grounds that he was the "14th Earl of Home" (Lord Home got his own back by reminding the leader of the opposition that he was the 14th Mr Wilson), but there is something undeniably romantic about being able to trace one's family back to the thirteenth century (Lord Mowbray is the 27th Lord Segrave), and Lady Sutherland, one of five countesses in their own right, derives her title from an even earlier creation than that of Segrave, patented in 1235.

The Life Peerage Act of 1958 was in part a half-hearted attempt to rid the House of Lords of its hereditary principle, and thus its unrepresentative and totally undemocratic nature. Despite Mrs Thatcher's recent breach of the spirit that has since prevailed, no hereditary peerages having been created between 1964-83,[4] and notwithstanding her decision to recommend no peerages of any kind in the 1984 Birthday Honours List, for those who desire a peerage their best hope still lies in a life peerage rather than a hereditary one. Life peers were not in fact invented by the 1958 Act; the Lords of Appeal

---

4. Although the last hereditary peerages were announced on New Year's Day 1965, they were gazetted 1964, the year of offer and acceptance.

in Ordinary (the Law Lords), with their retired colleagues, have sat as life peers since 1876, and the twenty-six Anglican bishops who take a seat in the House of Lords in order of seniority do so as a form of life peer, relinquishing their peerage on retirement from their see. Including the bishops and nine Lords of Appeal in Ordinary there are now some 365 life peers. There is no limit to the number of new life peers who may be created at any time; like hereditary peers, they are elevated by the sovereign on the advice of the prime minister, take the style and dignity of barons, and their children, like all the children of life peers since 1876 (but not the children of bishops), are accorded the style of "Honourable".

At the present time the peerage consists of about 850 hereditary peers of the realm, some 365 life peers and nearly 200 peers bearing courtesy titles. Together with their brothers and their sisters and their cousins and their aunts they are intended to cosset the sovereign — under the British Constitution, when in Council "the fountain of honour" and specifically charged with "increasing the peerage" — and in a very special way, for a monarch floating around on his or her own, entirely divorced by culture and social standing from every subject, is thought to be not only a very lonely person but a very vulnerable one. To rule in the past with the consent and help of those who in turn maintained the land and controlled the population was never an infallible model for monarchies but it seemed to offer the best hope of stability. It was from the hierarchical principle of social stratification that most western forms of government evolved, and in its context, the hereditary system was perfectly plausible. You fought for yourself and expected the spoils to pass to your son. The hereditary principle was never called into question until the commons had acquired enough influence in economic affairs to encourage them to claim a permanent influence in Parliament. The earliest forms of peerage, the earldoms bestowed by King Canute and the baronies brought over from Normandy and extended by William I and his successors, were distributed in the main to landowners whose allegiance the king required in the matter of government, and if necessary, war. The conferment of a peerage was never, as it was later to become, simply an honour for its own sake. A peerage was in some cases a reward for loyalty, the concrete reward being the land, the title quite literally "the title to the land" (Earl of Northumberland, Earl of Westmorland, Earl of Surrey), but the essential purpose of the peerage was the building up of a reliable and self-generating "family" of advisers to the king, men who could meet him almost on an equal footing, and even when ties of blood were absent the sovereign frequently addressed peers as Cousin. In Shakespeare's *Henry V* the king refers to the Earl of Westmorland as his "fair cousin", and even today in official documents the sovereign addresses peers of the realm as her "trusty and beloved cousin". Royalty are so short of social equals and intimate friends that Queen Victoria habitually addressed the King of Prussia, father-in-law of her eldest daughter, as "Sire, my most honoured brother" and signed herself "In true friendship Your Majesty's sincerely devoted Sister," and George V signed letters to the Austrian ambassador, Count Mensdorff, "Your affectionate friend and cousin," although, through shared descent from the Prince Consort's grandfather, the count was in fact no more than the king's second cousin once removed.

CHAPTER THREE

Second-Class Peers

I have recently been enjoying the delights of The Complete Baronetage *(shortly to be reissued in a single volume at the give-away price of £75 . . .) and have come to the conclusion that there is much to be said for Sir Walter Elliot's habit of never taking up "any book but the Baronetage".*

Mr Hugh Montgomery-Massingberd, *writing in the* Spectator, *18 December 1982.*

Within the British honours system there has been, for the past 350 years, a much coveted and frequently purchased title outside the peerage but carrying hereditary status, the baronetage. In the form in which we know it today the baronetage dates from 1611. The recipient is styled "Sir John Smith", and to differentiate a baronet from a knight it is customary to write "Bt" after the bearer's name — or "Bart", to which, however, most baronets object. It has been argued that by letters patent James I, in 1611, was reconstituting a term first applied to those peers who had lost their rights of individual summons to Parliament, and indeed the word "baronet" does carry the clear connotation of "lesser baron". If this historical root is correct, "baronets" can in fact be traced back to a statute of Richard II. Yet it seems there were even earlier references to baronets, or bannerets, fighting at the Battle of Barrenberg in 1321, and of Edward II creating eight "baronets" in 1328. Between the reigns of Richard II and

James I there seem also to have been baronets of some sort created, in 1446 and 1551, but it is thought unlikely the title was at that time hereditary. Even the spelling of the word baronet took over a century to settle down into common usage after James I's creation of the modern baronet; Sir Robert Dryden, who died in 1708, is described on his tomb in the church at Canons Ashby in Northamptonshire as a "Barronett".

James I, always in need of money and greatly attached to patronage, has frequently been credited, if that is the right word, with hitting on the idea of offering for sale a hereditary title, with no seat in the House of Lords attached, in order to finance the garrisoning of Ulster. While it is perfectly true that James sold the first 200 baronetcies — and his son, Charles I, even more desperate than his father for funds and friends, a further 458 — the original idea of creating the new order actually came from Parliament, composed to a large extent of men who had seen in the past eight years the House of Lords topped up with *nouveaux riches* who had purchased their titles, and the pavements of London become congested with knights who had done nothing more than catch the king's fancy. Parliament felt the need for some new honour that would bridge the gap between tuppeny ha'penny knights (they had existed in Falstaff's time) and the old landed families. Francis Bacon, the Lord Chancellor, first proposed the idea in principle of a new title in 1606, and three years later Sir Robert Cotton produced a report on ways of increasing revenue, which included among its recommendations the sale of titles. By 1611 the government had formulated plans to sell 100 baronetcies for £100 each, James accepted the idea, and the cost shot up to £1,095, the sum required to maintain thirty infantrymen in Ulster for three years. A further £1,200 was required for the patent. The new baronets were expected to have an income of at least £1,000 a year, and James promised never to let their numbers rise above 200.

So much for good intentions. Almost everything backfired. There was an initial scramble to become the first baronet, a race fairly easily won, we may assume, by Nicholas Bacon, for

Second-Class Peers

he happened to be the brother of the Lord Chancellor. His descendant, Sir Edmund Bacon, who has also collected the Garter and the KBE, is therefore the premier baronet of England. Bacon lined up on 22 May 1611, together with seventeen other "gentlemen of the first quality", but then all hell broke loose when the new hereditary baronets discovered they were not, as the king had promised, to take precedence immediately after the barons but after the barons' younger sons. This vital matter of precedence — the whole hierarchical system of society depended upon it — was only resolved after an ill-tempered three-day meeting of the Privy Council. The king himself presided on the last day, remarking in exasperation at one moment, "Though I am Kinge of men yett I am not Kinge of time, and I growe olde with this." He came down in favour of the younger sons of barons, but tried to sweeten a bitter pill for the baronets by granting their eldest sons the right of knighthood on their twenty-first birthday, one of James's many peculiarities that must have failed to amuse Queen Victoria; it was a custom George IV discontinued when granting new baronetcies but failed to cancel retrospectively, and as late as 1874 the Queen found herself, at Windsor, bestowing a scarcely deserved knighthood upon the son and heir of Sir James Cotter.

The result of this unseemly wrangle over privilege, lost by the new baronets, coupled with the high cost of purchasing the title, meant that between 1612-14 no new takers came forward at all, and despite a reduction in the charge in 1614 to £666, it took the king eleven years to dispose of his original 200 baronetcies. By 1614 the new order had become so unpopular, among other reasons because "manie of the Barronets & their descendants beinge meanely descended have precidence before gentlemen of auntient familyes," that a vigorous attempt was made in Parliament to scrap the whole wretched business. It was soon flourishing again, however, but not as lucratively as the king had hoped; between 1619-22 the price of a baronetcy fell from £700 to £200, for the simple reason that the king and Buckingham had offered over 100 baronetcies in five years. And as the price fell so did the standing of the purchasers. In 1623 a Shropshire baronet, Sir Thomas Harris, a draper who had risen from the yeoman class, was accused by the Earl Marshal's court of "basenes and other bad qualities". This may have meant no more than a certain lack of finesse in the matter of table manners, for the verdict was that he was "declared and pronounced no gentleman". Indeed, "basenes" remained a characteristic of the conduct if not the breeding of many of the descendants of the early baronets. Sir Wolstan Dixie of Bosworth Hall, an "abandoned brutal rascal" in the opinion of Samuel Johnson, had a notorious reputation for physical violence. When he was presented to George II at a levee as Sir Wolstan Dixie of Bosworth Park, the king, vaguely recalling something to do with Richard II, said, "Bosworth, Bosworth! Big battle at Bosworth, wasn't it?" "Yes, Sir," replied Sir Wolstan, "but I thrashed him." Yet the charge against Harris of baseness was more serious than it sounds today, for to set out to prove that a man was not a gentleman was not impertinence but an attempt to establish a fact; a gentleman rated in the social hierarchy, and the court was saying that Sir Thomas had become a baronet before becoming a gentleman, a topsy-turvy state of affairs sufficient to throw the whole hierarchical system into confusion.

King James was often foolish but he was seldom dishonest, and he kept his pledge to restrict the new order of baronet to 200. As soon as his father was dead, however, Charles I entrusted a further distribution of eighty-five baronetcies to the Duke and Duchess of Buckingham and to Buckingham's mother. The Earls of Holland and Warwick also rode round Essex selling baronetcies, and before long the price had slipped to £200. Buckingham's murder put a brake on sales for a decade, but in 1641 the king, by now beset with enemies of his own making, again reneged on his father's undertaking, and within two years he had brought a further 128 families into the folds of the baronetage.

Like hereditary peerages, the baronetage soon became entangled in anomalies. In 1635 Charles I gave a baronetcy to a woman, Mary Bolles, and between 1664-1706 four Scottish baronetcies were created with remainder through the female line, one of which, Dalyell of the Binns, has been inherited but disowned by the Old Etonian Labour MP, Mr Tam Dalyell. (There have been some even quainter appellations than the Binns: in 1872 Field Marshal Pollock became Sir George Pollock of the Khyber Pass.) By the reign of George III, the baronetcy was a recognized reward for political services, which in the eighteenth century meant lending support to the king against his political opponents; and before he totally lost his reason the king even exceeded Charles I's bestowal of baronetcies by creating 525. Doctors were later to become favoured recipients. Queen Victoria gave a baronetcy to her surgeon-general, an example followed by Edward VII, whose life was actually twice saved by his doctors, five of whom became baronets. Despite the penchant of some for killing their patients, doctors had sometimes previously been knighted. One such was Charles II's doctor, Sir John Floyer, perhaps because he passionately believed in the power of the monarch's touch as a cure for the King's evil. He was later the childhood physician of Dr Johnson. By 1905 one of the Heralds of the Royal College was bemoaning the fact that "not one in six of the newly created baronets have any Arms at all", for by this time, under Edward's patronage, doctors were being followed by the ultimate *bête noire* of the aristocracy, industrialists, many of whom, men like Guinness, Coleman, Palmer, Morris, Lever and Wills, became, through the power of advertising, household names.

King Edward's interest in the distribution of baronetcies seems to have been stirred even before he became king. Quite improperly, he made representations to Gladstone in 1881 on behalf of four of his cronies, prompting a slightly ambiguous entry in the diary of Gladstone's secretary, Edward Hamilton, who wrote: "It is perhaps hardly fair to say so but these recommendations have rather an ugly look about them." One of Edward's supplicants was a wealthy builder called C. J. Freake, the only one of the four, according to Hamilton, "known to ordinary fame", in other words, of whom anyone had even heard. Hamilton thought a knighthood would have been quite sufficient for Freake, yet the Prince of Wales "persistently and somewhat questionably (if not fishily)" pressed Freake's name on the prime minister. The reason for this is more than hinted at in passages in Hamilton's diary that deserve to be treated with caution, for they bear the hallmarks of second-hand and hearsay evidence, yet if true they show the prince (who was certainly prone to getting involved in unfortunate scandals) in a very shady light indeed: "A respectable clergyman [the Reverend H.W. Bellairs] wrote not long since to say that he was in possession of information to which he could swear, that there were certain persons scheming for hereditary honours, and bribes to people in very high life . . . that a gentleman told him that he had been offered a baronetcy by the Prince of Wales . . . on condition that he would pay £70,000 to the Prince's agent on receiving the title." Very rich men (the Prince of Wales had an annual income of £100,000 at a time when taxation was minute and the cost of living incredibly low) are sometimes tempted to become even richer; in more recent times Prince Bernhard of the Netherlands, married to the richest woman in the world, allowed himself to be socially ruined by accepting bribes. For the prince to have contemplated taking bribes would have been an immensely risky undertaking (as it was for Prince Bernhard, yet he still fell for the temptation), especially if he was supposed to be receiving the money through an "agent", whoever any such person may have been. It is perfectly possible that the prince had gambling debts; what is absolutely certain is that two financial burdens he bore were the cost of renovating Sandringham House, estimated at £80,000, and his wife's legendary extravagance, and between 1863-67 the prince's expenditure had exceeded his income by a total of £100,000. So by 1881 he could well have been desperate. Yet by that time he had immensely wealthy friends, some of whom would have thought it an honour to bail him out for nothing, and although Hamilton's diary entries are damaging, and the supporting circumstantial evidence relating to the prince's finances is strong, in the absence of concrete proof of guilt

Second-Class Peers

King Edward deserves the benefit of the doubt, and hence a formal acquittal.

As with the peerage, the baronetcy also became used as a method of perpetuating famous names. The ball was set rolling by George III when in 1760 he awarded a baronetcy to a boy of 9, Charles Watson, in recognition of his father's services as an admiral. The heroic deeds of General Sir Henry Lawrence, mortally wounded at the Battle of Lucknow, were similarly commemorated by his 17-year-old son being made a baronet. The baronetcy held by Sir Robert Lucas-Tooth became extinct when his three sons were all killed in the First World War, so although his nephew only rejoiced in the name of Warrand, he changed his name by deed poll, was made a baronet, and became Sir Hugh Lucas-Tooth. The Second World War, too, saw the baronetcy brought into the centre of controversy: such doubts had been stirred up over the deployment of Bomber Command by Marshal of the Royal Air Force Sir Arthur Harris that at the end of the war he was passed over for the viscountcy he might well have expected, and had to wait eight years, for Churchill's return to power, to be compensated with a baronetcy.

Clement Attlee had in fact recommended precisely seven baronetcies in six years, five of them for Lord Mayors of London; within a year of winning the 1951 general election, Churchill had sent the names of ten new baronets to the Palace. The Lord Mayor of London had first been made a baronet in 1641, and between 1889-1962 it became the almost invariable custom for the annual inhabitant of the Mansion House to be given a baronetcy. This was regarded as some sort of recompense for the enormous sum the Lord Mayor is obliged to spend out of his own pocket, on top of his official expenses, during his year of office, for the Lord Mayor of London lives and entertains in regal splendour. With the cessation of new hereditary peerages in 1964, no new baronets have been created, but since Mrs Thatcher's cautious resurrection of hereditary peerages in 1983 there is in theory no reason now why new baronets should not be created too.

What has happened in recent years in the case of Lord Mayors, most of them already knights, is that they have been advanced from Knight Commander to Knight Grand Cross, and in the case of Lady Donaldson, Lord Mayor from 1983-4 and with no previous title in her own right, she was made a Dame Grand Cross of the Order of the British Empire. Her successor as Lord Mayor of London, Sir Alan Traill, most unusually had no knighthood when he was elected in 1984, and his appointment as a GBE was announced in *The Times,* under "Latest Appointments", alongside that of a new parliamentary private secretary. Certain other offices also almost invariably carry a knighthood; examples include the Solicitor-General, the Attorney-General and High Court Judges, but one luckless registrar of the Privy Council's Judicial Committee, Henry Reeve, was deprived of his customary knighthood by Queen Victoria for daring to edit the memoirs of Charles Greville, Clerk of the Privy Council from 1821-59.

Unless future prime ministers do recommend new baronetcies, the order is almost bound to become extinct one day — probably, in fact, by about the year 2154, for including the 200-odd baronetcies held by peers, there are at present around 1,342 proven baronetcies, and they are becoming extinct at the rate of eight a year. At least two baronets in recent times have gone missing, Sir Herbert Bartlett, in 1921, in best Agatha Christie style, by vanishing overnight during a crossing from Dover to Ostend, and the Earl of Lucan, wanted, if alive, for questioning in connection with the murder of his children's nanny. The objection to creating new baronets, quite apart from any overriding arguments there may be against new hereditary titles in general, is that the recipients seem somehow like second-class peers, men thought worthy of hereditary status yet somehow not quite fit to sit in the House of Lords. Backbench politicians have often fallen into this category, and one of the most extraordinary examples must surely be that of Mr Arthur du Cros. The Countess of Warwick, one of Edward VII's most famous mistresses, finding herself beset by debts, allowed it to be known that she possessed letters from the late king which she was prepared to sell for £100,000. George V managed to slap an injunction on her through the High Court, forbidding the sale of the letters in Great Britain, but lest Lady Warwick should then find a purchaser in America, du Cros, a Conservative member of Parliament and the founder of the Dunlop Rubber Company, settled her debts to the tune of £64,000. After a respectable interval of time — in 1916 in fact — he became Sir Arthur du Cros, Bt.

CHAPTER FOUR

Knights and Dames

I like the Garter; there's no damned merit in it.
                                                Lord Melbourne.

If the system of distributing honours for their own sake has any discernible roots they lie in the development of the various orders of knighthood, for it needs to be remembered that knighthood was an honour quite separate from the peerage and might be conferred upon someone (as it is today) who already held a peerage. Since the falling into abeyance in 1922 of the Most Illustrious Order of St Patrick, founded in 1783 by George III, and the granting of independence to India in 1947, when the Most Exulted Order of the Star of India ceased to be awarded, there remain half a dozen orders of knighthood, that of knight bachelor, although often thought of as the least desirable, being the oldest. The rather strange appellation "bachelor" is thought by some historians to have been attached to the order by Henry III, to indicate that unlike a peerage, the title was non-hereditary, and the title "knight" itself derives from the Saxon word *cnyht*, a servant or attendant.

Modern concepts of knighthood are firmly embedded in what today we think of as the age of chivalry, the years of the twelfth to fourteenth centuries, while much of its mythology rests upon far earlier tales of King Arthur, the round table, Camelot in Somerset, dragons, and maidens in distress. In his book on chivalry,[1] Maurice Keen traces the origins of knighthood, so frequently identified with St Michael, St George and the Crusades, to the pagan warrior caste of pre-Christian Europe, when adulthood was marked by the wearing of arms. The sword certainly seems always to have been crucial to knighthood, and although in later times a new knight would have his sword blessed by a priest or bishop, he was girded by the king or a peer. A man might be knighted in the field of battle for valour, since to some extent knighthood, for the aristocracy, took the place for many centuries of the far later invention of decorations, but the dubbing of a young man on the shoulder with a sword more frequently, and certainly throughout the age of chivalry, indicated that he was now fit to pursue the life of a knight, which meant behaving with courtesy and honour. A knight who failed to live up to expectations could expect to have his spurs ripped off and his insides ripped out. When a knight is unmasked as a traitor today, the Queen still reserves the right, even though she may have known of his treachery while it was kept a secret from the rest of the world, to strip him of his knighthood, as she did with Professor Anthony Blunt in 1979.

Sir Roger Casement too was stripped of his knighthood, before being executed for treason. To abolish a peerage, an Act of Parliament is required, and when Lord Kagan, who had received a life peerage in Harold Wilson's controversial 1976 Resignation Honours List, was sent to prison for fraud and theft, he was stripped only of his knighthood, also conferred, in 1970, under Mr Wilson's patronage. His firm, the Gannex textile group, lost its royal warrant. Anything the Crown gives, the Crown, it seems, can take away, but decisions seem to be fairly arbitrary. William Pottinger, a civil servant sent to prison for corruptly receiving gifts from the architect John Poulson, lost both his CB and CVO. When a member of Parliament was accused of illegal sexual conduct with boys his imminent peerage was cancelled; when a retired diplomat became identified with the Paeodophile Information

1. *Chivalry* (New Haven, Yale University Press, 1984).

Knights and Dames

Exchange, he retained his knighthood. Few in the House of Commons or the Political Honours Scrutiny Committee could have been unaware of Tom Driberg's predilection for homosexual adventures in the corridors of the Palace of Westminster, yet he was sent to the House of Lords.

A knight has always been styled "Sir John Smith", and for the past three or four hundred years his wife "Lady Smith", but certainly well into the sixteenth century the wife of a knight was alternatively known as "Dame Anne Smith". The title Dame is today reserved for those women who receive the equivalent of a knighthood within the Most Honourable Order of the Bath, the Most Distinguished Order of St Michael & St George, the Royal Victorian Order or the Most Excellent Order of the British Empire. In 1926 a badge was instituted for knights bachelor to wear on a neck ribbon, commemorating the order's origins in chivalry by bearing an upright sword between two spurs. The cost to the new knight of his badge was £56, but in 1975 the Queen decided to make a gift of it.

The most prestigious order of knighthood is the Most Noble Order of the Garter. There are three reasons for this. With the exception of the Order of Knights Bachelor, it is the oldest, founded by Edward III at Windsor, in about the year 1348. The exact date has been disputed, but the official year of the order's foundation was settled by George VI when he celebrated its sexcentenary in 1948. Excluding the sovereign and other royalty, the order is restricted to twenty-four members. And whereas in the eighteenth century the Garter had slipped into the patronage of the prime minister, thus being awarded for party political services (Melbourne thought it so debased in his time that he declined it), Clement Attlee, with Churchill's approval, in 1946 restored the Garter to the Crown. There had been a broad hint dropped in 1912, when Sir Edward Grey — "the worst Foreign Secretary England ever had", in the biased opinion of Queen Alexandra — received the Garter, to the effect that the monarch would like to regain control of this almost sacred order; Lord Knollys, private secretary to George V, spotted that the prime minister's office were planning to announce that the king had "approved" the award, and he wrote asking that the word should be deleted. "He is supposed to be the Fountain of Honour", Asquith's secretary was somewhat plaintively reminded. Edward VII had placed so much importance upon bestowal of the Garter that when he came to present it to one of his close friends, Lord Carrington, he donned Field Marshal's uniform for the occasion and broke with tradition by making a little speech. "I was so much moved," Carrington recorded in his journal, "that I left the Garter behind." Royal mythology abounds with tales relating to Edward VII and his meticulous obsession with orders and decorations. Apparently he received a shock one evening at Devonshire House when he discovered the duke himself wearing the Garter upside down, and on a visit to the duke's country house, Chatsworth, the king had occasion to point out to another guest, Sir Felix Semon, that the Star of the Royal Victorian Order was *usually* worn on the *left* breast".

The Garter is now one of four honours remaining in the exclusive gift of the sovereign; the others are the Order of the Thistle (like the Garter, returned to the Crown by Clement Attlee, in 1947), the Order of Merit and the Royal Victorian Order. Some of the current knights companions of the Garter may seem dull and unimaginative choices to the public, but it is no longer necessarily the public they have served, and it has to be remembered that even a prime minister who is offered and accepts the Garter, and may consistently over a number of years have antagonized half the population, has performed, day in and day out, a very personal service to the sovereign. By exercising patronage over the Garter the Queen is also enabled, should she wish, to recognize and reward some slightly quirky person whose public life has caught her fancy but who might not be recommended for an honour by the prime minister. Bestowal of the Garter in 1971 on the Earl of Longford, a run-of-the-mill publisher and a not very successful politician, was surely the Queen's way of showing support for his stand on public morals.

The award of the Garter has also been one method used of perpetuating a kind of *crème de la crème* within the ruling élite; at least twenty-five out of thirty-eight Beauforts,

Marlboroughs, Northumberlands and Salisburys have received the order, and while in the hands of the prime minister it also sometimes became a pawn in international policy making. Anxious to have Persia on Great Britain's side rather than Russia's, Arthur Balfour wanted Edward VII to give the Garter to the Shah in 1902. The king protested — not very convincingly, for his mother had bestowed the Garter on the Shah's father, and on two Sultans of Turkey — that it was a Christian order, and refused. But his Minister for Foreign Affairs, Lord Lansdowne, was under the clear impression that the king had nodded his consent, and even had the brainwave of getting a special Star designed omitting the Christian cross of St George. On board the royal yacht, King Edward opened a Foreign Office box, discovered Lansdowne's truncated design, flew into one of his famous rages and hurled it through the porthole. It fell into a stream pinnace and was retrieved by a stoker. Things got even more out of hand when Lansdowne admitted he had virtually promised the Garter to the Shah, and said that if the king would not confer it, he would feel obliged to resign. Eventually the king simmered down and the Shah got his Garter, complete with cross.

The conferment of the Garter on another head of state, Kaiser William II, was later to cause anxiety to George V, who came under considerable pressure during the First World War to have his wretched cousin's Garter banner removed from the Chapel at Windsor Castle. "Although as a rule I never interfere, I think the time has come when I must speak out," his mother, Queen Alexandra, wrote to him. "It is but right and proper for you to have down those hateful German banners in our sacred Church." Reluctantly, for much though he loathed the war and detested many of Germany's unchivalrous actions he did not believe in trying to rewrite history, the king agreed. "Otherwise," he explained to a friend, "the people would have stormed the Chapel."

Part of the fun of getting the Garter is all the dressing up it entails. The garter itself, from which the order takes its name, is dark velvet, bears the famous and frequently mistranslated motto "*Honi soit qui mal y pense*" (Shame on him who thinks evil of it), and is worn by men below the left knee and by ladies (there are at present three, Queen Elizabeth the Queen Mother, the Queen of Denmark and Princess Juliana of the Netherlands) above the left elbow. There is a mantle of blue velvet, with the badge of the order embroidered on the left breast, a hood of crimson velvet, a surcoat of crimson velvet lined with taffeta and a hat of black velvet with a plume of ostrich feathers fastened to it with a diamond badge. Once all that lot is on, the knights decorate themselves with a gold collar, to which is attached the George, a figure of the saint, patron and protector of the order, made of gold enamel. The oval Badge, known as the Lesser George, again made of gold, is worn on the right hip, suspended from a dark blue Broad Ribbon, worn, unusually for British orders, over the left shoulder. (The Thistle too is worn over the left shoulder, and St Patrick used to be.) On the left breast (all British Stars are worn on the left) reposes the eight-pointed Star of the Order. Each knight has his own stall in the chapel at Windsor Castle, above which hangs his banner, places the letters KG after his name, and when he dies his nearest male relative is received in audience and hands the insignia back to the sovereign. Also returnable to the sovereign personally is the insignia of the Thistle. The collars of the other orders of chivalry, together with the Royal Victorian Chain, are returnable to the Central Chancery of the Orders of Knighthood. Not every insignia of the Garter has been retrieved, however. Kitchener's went down with him when he was drowned in HMS *Hampshire* in 1916, and in her book of reminiscences, Princess Marie Louise, a granddaughter of Queen Victoria, recalled being shown on a visit to Stratfield Saye the Badge of the Garter worn at the time of his execution by Charles I, handed by the king for safe keeping to Bishop Juxon, and now in the possession of the Duke of Wellington.[2] Sir Winston Churchill's insignia is on loan from the Queen at Chartwell.

2. *My Memories of Six Reigns* (London, Evans Bros, 1956). The Badge was recovered by Charles II at the Restoration. James II took it into exile. It descended to the Countess of Albany, widow of the Young Pretender, who sold it in 1811 to Marquess Wellesley, elder brother of the 1st Duke of

Knights and Dames

Even more select in numbers than the knights companions of the Garter are the knights of the Most Ancient and Most Noble Order of the Thistle, who number at any time no more than sixteen. Legend has it that the order crossed the border with James I, but it was not until the reign of James II that St Giles's Cathedral in Edinburgh was designated the chapel of the order. Although the exact origins of the Thistle remain obscure, it is certainly known that the original intention was to restrict membership to Scottish nobles. But English peers have been eligible since the reign of George I, and in 1965 the Queen admitted a commoner, Sir James Robertson. Knights of the Thistle place the letters KT after their name.

Perhaps more wet jokes have been made about the Most Honourable Order of the Bath than any other order within the honours system, but the truth is that the order did have its origins in the custom of young men taking a communal bath (not a common occurrence in the Middle Ages, and more concerned with a symbolic cleansing of the spirit than a scrubbing of the body) on the eve of receiving knighthood. Mention is made by the long-lived medieval chronicler Jean Froissart[3] of 46 esquires bathing in 1399 the night before the coronation of Henry IV, in preparation for their own knighting. Queen Elizabeth I created 11 knights of the Bath at her coronation in 1559 but by the time of her death, in 1603, with no similar functions to celebrate, like royal marriages or christenings, the order was nearly extinct, so James I created 62 at his coronation. Further transitions and vicissitudes eventually resulted in the order being officially dated from 1725, the year in which it was revived by George I as a military order. In 1815 the Prince Regent separated the order into three classes, knights grand cross, knights commanders and companions, and in 1847 Queen Victoria admitted civil knights and companions.

The Prince Regent, whose passion for military parades was

Wellington, to whom it was bequeathed. Lord Wellesley quite improperly bequeathed his own Garter insignia to Alfred Montgomery, his private secretary and very possibly also his illegitimate son.
3. 1327-1410; he came to England in 1360 from Hainault.

The Honours System

only exceeded by his love of dressing up, instituted in 1818 a new order of chivalry, the Most Distinguished Order of St Michael & St George. Like the Bath, St Michael & St George is divided into three classes, thus allowing to be admitted to the order members who are not considered distinguished enough to be knights. Or not yet, for the majority of recipients of the CMG are primarily junior diplomats and civil servants working their way up the ladder, with a little encouragement from the honours system on the way. The same advantage works through the class-orientated mechanism of the Order of the Bath: a brigadier may expect a CB, and then a KCB on promotion to lieutenant-general and the GCB when he is appointed Chief of the Imperial General Staff. The mandarins of the Foreign Office have Queen Victoria to thank for their eligibility for membership of the Order of St Michael & St George. It was originally intended for the inhabitants of Malta, ceded to Britain in 1814 by the Treaty of Paris, and for the inhabitants of the Ionian Islands, placed under British protection at the same time but in 1863 ceded to Greece. Sixteen years later, Queen Victoria decided to revive a purpose of the order by admitting anyone who had rendered distinguished service in connection with foreign affairs, and eventually the order was extended to anyone who had served in relation to any part of the British Dominions, which is why today recipients figure so prominently in the Diplomatic and Overseas List.

Because of the exclusive patronage of the sovereign, one of the most prized of the orders of knighthood is the Royal Victorian Order. It was instituted in 1896 by Queen Victoria, somewhat late in her reign, one might think, as a means of rewarding those who had rendered any personal service to the sovereign or to other members of the Royal Family, and certainly it must have been some small compensation for the hours of tedium involved when in waiting, especially in the freezing cold of Balmoral. Even so, the ladies-in-waiting and housekeepers were excluded, for Victoria created the order specifically for men. One of the few positive initiatives taken by Edward VIII was to extend the Royal Victorian Order to women. Certain services rewarded with the Royal Victorian Order have been more personal than others, and few as personal as those rendered by Sir Rufus Isaccs and Sir John Simon when they were Attorney-General and Solicitor-General respectively, and helped to settle successfully a libel case resulting from an accusation of bigamy against George V. They were both made KCVO. Victoria had, however, instituted a medallion of herself and Prince Albert, the Royal Victoria and Albert, in 1862, exclusively for women. It conferred no title and was merely intended as something pretty to wear attached to a bow. The last holder, Princess Alice, Countess of Athlone, a granddaughter of Queen Victoria, died in 1981, and it can be presumed that no more of these mementoes, so highly personal to Queen Victoria, will be awarded.

Although excluding women from the Royal Victorian Order, Queen Victoria had admitted women to the Imperial Order of the Crown of India from its inception in 1877, and women have also been eligible for the Order of Merit, the Order of the Companions of Honour and the Order of the British Empire from inception. But they had to wait until 1965 for admittance to the Order of St Michael & St George and until 1971 to the Order of the Bath. There is some controversy as to whether women were ever admitted to the Order of the Garter, but attendance by women at medieval feasts of the order is not regarded by modern researchers (including Mr Cyril Hankinson, for forty years editor of *Debrett's*) to have constituted full membership. Queen Alexandra was the first Lady of the Garter, admitted by Edward VII. Ladies of the Garter are invariably of royal blood or married to royalty, and are admitted as extra members, not as dames.

So exalted are some of those who may expect to receive the Royal Victorian Order (the Master of the Horse, for instance), and so humble others (the botanist to Her Majesty's Household in Scotland, perhaps), that the order was divided into five divisions, members being split into fourth and fifth class, with the MVO fourth class being regarded as the equivalent of an OBE, the fifth class of an MBE. To

The Honours System

differentiate more clearly between the two MVO classes, the Queen decided that from 1 January 1985 members fourth-class would be designated "lieutenant", and the first lieutenant of the Royal Victorian Order, the Queen's press secretary, Mr Michael Shea, was invested on 14 February 1985. The Royal Victorian Order even has a medal in silver gilt, silver and bronze, thus enabling the entire hierarchy below stairs as well as above to be summoned to the drawing-room at Sandringham or Balmoral and have something appropriate to their station in life pinned on them.

A Knight Grand Cross of the order (the Lord Chamberlain, for instance, who deserves an award if only for being compelled, in the course of his duties, to walk backwards) places GCVO after his name, a Dame (perhaps a lady-in-waiting, who will have sacrificed months of family life to answering letters from schoolchildren and carrying umbrellas) DCVO, a knight commander (the private secretary or the Keeper of the Queen's Archives) KCVO, companions CVO, lieutenants LVO and members MVO. There is no limit to the numbers whom the Queen may admit to her private order, and on state visits she simply hands out awards to those who look as though they could do with them — an ambassador not yet knighted by the Foreign Office, or a first secretary who has co-ordinated the arrangements, who may be handed the CVO quite informally on the last night, together with a signed photograph in a silver frame and a pair of enamelled cufflinks. How the first secretary's CVO tallies with the MVO the Queen is likely to award to a retiring equerry to the Duke of Edinburgh only Her Majesty understands.

With no less than seven orders of knighthood (eight including knights bachelor) already in existence — for at that time the Order of St Patrick, of which the last holder was Prince Henry, Duke of Gloucester, and the Star of India were still on offer — in 1917 George V decided to give a boost to patriotism by instituting the Most Excellent Order of the British Empire, initially intended for services rendered to the Empire other than of a military nature. As his grandmother Queen Victoria had done when instituting the Royal Victorian

Order, he opened it to members as well as officers and companions, thus eventually enabling postmistresses to receive a prize as well as colonels. Before they had finished, the king and queen had done quite a bit of tinkering with the order. In 1918 a military division was added, and shortly before his death the king had the central device of the Badge, originally depicting Britannia, changed to an effigy of himself and Queen Mary, and gave instructions that it was never to be changed again. Queen Mary did ask, however, that the colours of the military ribbon should be altered from purple with a scarlet stripe to rose-pink edged with grey. The Empire whose glory the order was established to reflect has long since become a Commonwealth, not all of whose members any longer permit their nationals to receive knighthood, and yet today the Order of the British Empire is the most widely distributed order in the honours system, a kind of safety net in which to catch all those who would otherwise fail to qualify for an honour of any kind, sport, the theatre, literature and the shires being liberally strewn twice a year with CBEs, OBEs and MBEs.

There is one category of subject for whom knighthood is a particularly sore subject — the Anglican clergy, or to be more precise, clergy wives. While a priest or bishop may be admitted to an order of chivalry he may not receive the accolade, for receipt of the accolade might involve the necessity to take up arms to defend the sovereign. Hence no clerical knight ever acquires the style of "Sir" and his wife can never be known as "Lady Smith". George V's decision to appoint his tiresome old tutor, Canon John Dalton, a KCVO gave expression to one of Sir Frederick Ponsonby's many amusing epistles on court life. "The question," he wrote, "whether Mrs Dalton, wife of Canon Dalton, KCVO, should take precedence of Lady Parratt, wife of Sir Walter Parratt, Knight Bachelor [Parratt was Master of the King's Music], had shaken Windsor to its foundations, but as it had never been officially settled even the strongest refrained from inviting these two ladies to meet at dinner." Not surprisingly, as the Great War was in progress at the time, Sir Frederick added, "In order to appreciate the subtleties of this question, it is necessary to wade in depths of vulgarity which have rarely been plumbed before." In 1949 the Reverend Robert Hyde was offered a knighthood, chose to receive the accolade and was obliged by Archbishop Fisher to resign holy orders. Another debarment peculiar to the Anglican clergy is from membership of the House of Commons.

The Royal Victorian Chain is another gift the Queen has at her personal disposal. Instituted in 1902 by Edward VII, it carries no title or precedence, and is useful for bestowing on heads of state who already possess the Garter (Princess Juliana of the Netherlands received the Chain in 1950, the King of Norway in 1955), and in 1974, instead of giving the retiring archbishop of Canterbury the KCVO, fairly frequently bestowed on senior clergy, the Queen decided to present Lord Ramsey (and in 1980, Lord Coggan) with the Royal Victorian Chain.

One might think that in a nation as loyal to the Crown as Britain no one would ever decline, or make a fuss about receiving, the KCVO, but during the reign of George V the twin daughters of Major-General Lord Ruthven were refused admittance to the royal enclosure at Ascot because they were actresses, and their indignant father refused the KCVO he was offered as General Officer Commanding London District. The same sovereign offered the KCVO to an arch-collector of honours, Sir Edward Elgar, already a knight bachelor, who promptly wrote to a friend, Lady Stuart of Wortley, to say, "H.M. has offered me the wretched *KCVO* (!!!) which awful thing I must accept! Alas!" Harold Nicolson accepted a commission to write the official life of George V and must have known perfectly well that on publication he would be offered a KCVO, but according to his wife's biographer, "They were not very pleased; they even thought of turning it down. It depressed them because the honour, so far from being an honour, seemed to them dreary and middle-class."[4] Nicolson had such an inflated opinion of himself he even wrote to Vita

4. *Vita: The Life of V. Sackville-West* by Victoria Glendinning (London, Weidenfeld & Nicolson, 1983).

Sackville-West: "If I had never been given anything I should have retained my potential repute; being assessed so low diminishes my prestige." The truth is, both he and Elgar ached for a peerage. The Nicolsons gave instructions to their servants to continue to call them Mr and Mrs Nicolson, and Vita even dropped "The Hon" from envelopes to Harold (he was the younger son of Lord Carnock) and took to addressing him as "Harold Nicolson". She detested being addressed by anyone as Lady Nicolson. The gift of a knighthood from King George VI, it seems, was simply not good enough for the daughter of Lord Sackville.

Knights of the Garter and the Thistle, and knights (and dames) grand cross, all of whom wear collars with their insignia, need to brush up on "collar days", the days on which the collar is worn: such galas as Christmas Day, various saints days and the Duke of Edinburgh's birthday. It is also useful to know that collars can be worn at the introduction of a new member of the House of Lords — but only before sunset, a stipulation which presumably explains why, apart from the fact that they would fail to get their photograph in the morning newspapers, new peers are never introduced at night. With morning dress, the collar should be held in position "with black cotton thread on a small gilt safety pin". Sir Frederick Ponsonby has recalled Lord Milner being soundly ticked off by the pompous Lord Curzon for wearing his Garter sash over his right shoulder at a levee, only to get his own back when Curzon arrived for a levee on a collar day, "committing the most heinous offence of wearing a riband *as well as* a collar. Of course, the King [George V] observed this at once but made little of it, only chaffing Curzon about the mistake; Milner, who was also present, heard these remarks and afterwards wrote to Curzon, repeating nearly word for word that it was almost inconceivable that anyone who had been given this ancient order etc. etc."[5]

There are two orders within the orders of chivalry other than knighthoods: the Order of Merit, founded by Edward VII in 1902, the same year that he founded the Royal Victorian

---
5. *Recollections of Three Reigns.*

Chain, and the Order of the Companions of Honour, a later and similar wartime invention of George V (similar in so far as it is often hard to understand the fine distinction that must presumably be drawn between merit and honour). Edward specifically intended the Order of Merit to be a personal award from the sovereign to anyone gaining outstanding and generally recognized distinction by means of military service, literature, science or art. Almost within minutes of instituting the order, King Edward received Lord Kitchener, on 12 July 1902, and invested him while lying in bed recovering from his operation for appendicitis. As the hero of the Boer War knelt by the king's bedside and kissed his hand, Queen Alexandra was overcome by her accustomed emotion and burst into tears. Excluding foreigners, the order is restricted to two dozen members, and in the course of eighty years it has been awarded to only four women: Florence Nightingale, the 1964 Nobel Prize winner for chemistry, Dorothy Hodgkin, the historian Veronica Wedgwood and Mother Teresa of Calcutta, the first honorary woman member, admitted by the Queen in 1984. The Queen also admitted both Professor Hodgkin (in 1965) and Dame Veronica (in 1969). Edward waited until 29 November 1907 to send the OM round to the home of Florence Nightingale, one of the greatest Englishwomen who has ever lived, when she was 87, blind and probably not fully aware of the honour. "Too kind," she murmured, "too kind."

George V showed considerable moral courage and a truly imaginative use of the royal prerogative when he bestowed the Order of Merit on Lord Haldane after he had been hounded from office as Lord Chancellor when irrational anti-German vilification was at its height during the First World War. When Kipling later declined the same honour, the king must have been hurt and a little surprised (hurt, too, perhaps, but surely not surprised when his offer of the OM was also spurned by Bernard Shaw). In fact it seems odd that Shaw should have been offered the OM at all, considering that in 1912 the king had a letter of complaint sent to Downing Street regarding the professed views of the naturalist Dr Alfred Wallace, whom Edward VII had appointed to the Order of Merit in 1908. "The King," Downing Street was told, "is rather scandalized that [a] possessor of the Order of Merit should avow himself to be a Socialist." A.E. Housman was another of the king's literary choices who declined the Order of Merit. Members of the order place OM after their name, and in the order of precedence they follow Knights Grand Cross of the Order of the Bath. Among their number today are Henry Moore, Sir Frederick Ashton, Lord Olivier and Sir Sidney Nolan.

The Order of the Companions of Honour, founded in 1917, consists of a maximum of sixty-five members. They rank after Knights Grand Cross of the Order of the British Empire, and some recipients get the Order of Merit too. Lord Clark had both. So did Churchill. Surprisingly, in view of his plebeian taste in music, George V suggested Delius for the CH in 1929. The order is a useful award for politicians, who seem to be getting something rather special without having to be sent to the House of Lords.

The great majority of honours are announced *en bloc*, in the two annual honours lists, published close to New Year's Day and on the Queen's official birthday, a Saturday in June agreed upon eighteen months in advance. There is also a coronation honours list, and on a rather more regular basis generally an honours list at the dissolution of Parliament. But the Queen may announce a new Knight of the Garter or member of the Order of Merit whenever a vacancy occurs, and to discover that someone has been received into the Royal Victorian Order it is often necessary to read the Court Circular. Awards for gallantry sometimes appear in the annual lists, but these too are quite often announced separately. At the head of this list resides the Victoria Cross. Awarded quite simply for "conspicuous bravery", the VC in fact takes precedence over all other honours excluding peerages, ranking even before the Garter. Those who hold the Victoria Cross are a classless band of the élite, in whose dwindling presence other individuals, regardless of their general opinions on war or honours, do well to give way and to keep their peace. There is no conceivable way in which a Victoria Cross can be canvassed for, purchased or in any other way debased. Until two Victoria Crosses were announced at the conclusion of the 1982 war in the Falklands, one of them awarded posthumously, only one award of the VC, to a lance-corporal in the Gurkha Rifles in 1965, had been made in the thirty-seven years since the end of the Second World War. Such are the feats of breathtaking heroism for which the VC is awarded, the wonder is that any recipient has ever lived to tell the tale.

For obvious reasons, most awards for gallantry have been presented by commanding officers in the field, but as often as possible the Victoria Cross is presented by the sovereign personally. After suffering a grievous riding accident while inspecting a detachment of the Royal Flying Corps in France in 1915, as a result of which he fractured his pelvis and three ribs and suffered excruciating pain, George V insisted on decorating Sergeant Oliver Brooks of the Coldstream Guards with the Victoria Cross before being taken to the hospital train. Queen Victoria, seated side-saddle and dressed in a black skirt and scarlet jacket, bent from her horse to bestow the first sixty-two crosses in Hyde Park on 26 June 1857, only eighteen months after the decoration had been instituted. Such a wholesale distribution may seem to smack of indifference to any question of degree of bravery, but it has to be remembered that at this date no other recognition for valour was available to privates, non-commissioned officers or junior officers (senior officers were eligible for companionship of the Order of the Bath). The invention of the Victoria Cross marked the moment when, thanks to the Crimean War, common soldiers ceased to be regarded as cannon fodder rounded up by the likes of Lord Cardigan, but were seen to be the equals of any peer of the realm in the face of the enemy. The Victoria Cross was quite simply the first decoration generally available for gallantry, and with the gradual extension of gallantry awards over the next fifty years, it acquired a more and more illustrious image as its award could be made increasingly sparingly. Only about seventy holders of the cross currently survive. They include privates, an army chaplain, a viscount and an admiral.

Once the Victoria Cross had been instituted as an award to be made irrespective of rank, new decorations for gallantry were incorporated into the honours system so as to differentiate between officers and other ranks, as if it were inconceivable that a butcher's boy from Bradford could behave as bravely at Ypres as a subaltern straight out of Wellington College. Class differentiation in awards for gallantry, perpetuated as each new award was instituted, in a kind of leap-frogging operation, had its unfortunate roots in the good intentions of Queen Victoria. After establishing the Victoria Cross as an award available for every rank, the queen realized that senior officers were still also eligible for the Bath, and wishing to do something for "Sergeants, Corporals and Privates of Our Army" she instituted, in 1862, the Distinguished Conduct Medal. It was not long before commissioned ranks felt they deserved a decoration of their own to match the DCM, so in 1886 the queen gave approval to the Distinguished Service Order. Then came the First World War. Strictly speaking, the DSO remains an order, not a decoration, although it is of course awarded to officers for personal acts of outstanding bravery, and sometimes to the colonel of a regiment or battalion in recognition of his regiment's outstanding role in some specific action. But in December 1914, by which time war had taken on a whole new dimension, it was felt that junior officers had been left out in the cold, and so the Military Cross was instituted, specifically for captains and first and second lieutenants.

The circumstances in which the now much valued and revered Military Cross was instituted and designed have been recorded with suitable zest and irony by a first-hand observer, Sir Frederick Ponsonby, and the account he gives in *Recollections of Three Reigns* is so amusing and informative it deserves to be quoted at length. He writes:

"I attended the meeting of the committee appointed to institute the new cross and found that it consisted of the Adjutant-General, the Military Secretary, the Secretary of the War Office, Douglas Dawson[6] and myself, with Kitchener in the chair.

"The word 'autocrat' can only give a feeble idea of what Kitchener was at that time. The War Office blindly carried out his orders, and no one ever thought of questioning his proposals or of attempting to argue with him. The committee was therefore a farce, as the officials of the War Office were like a Greek Chorus echoing his opinions. The only two who asked awkward questions and tried to get the subject thoroughly thrashed out were Douglas Dawson and myself. When we came to the design I suggested we should have something really good, but Kitchener said it would take too long and there was no necessity to have anything damned artistic. However, it was agreed to have as many designs as possible to choose from, or rather from which Kitchener might make his selection. I longed to say that not one of the committee had the slightest knowledge of silver work and therefore we were as a body totally incapable of selecting the best work; but I felt it would not do to say so, more especially as Kitchener seemed to fancy himself as an artist, and was constantly engaged in drawing pathetic designs on the blotting-paper.

"The second meeting of the committee took place soon afterwards, and in the short time available I was not able to do more than get one or two artists to draw rough sketches. Douglas Dawson, however, had asked Farnham Burke,[7] one of the leading Heralds, to draw designs. To my mind they were very second rate, but considerable trouble had been taken with them and silver paint had been used which I was afraid would captivate Kitchener. Sure enough, as soon as he saw Farnham Burke's efforts he refused even to look at the rough sketches, and at once selected the design with the silver paint. This was a triumph for Douglas Dawson, who from the first had been very strongly opposed to any artist

6. Brigadier-General Sir Douglas Dawson, Comptroller in the Lord Chamberlain's Office
7. Later Sir Henry Farnham Burke.

being employed, and he remarked to me that he was glad to think that the design he had put forward was the best; I retorted that so far from being the best it was probably the worst, as Kitchener knew as much about silver work as a Hindoo did about skates.

"The choosing of the ribbon was not without humour, as, everyone seemed to think it was such an easy thing to do. Kitchener began by describing a ribbon which he thought would be attractive, but I told him this was the Emperor of Austria's Jubilee Medal and, although this was not a serious objection, it was a pity to have a ribbon that was worn by nearly everyone in Austria. His second attempt produced the ribbon of the Conspicuous Gallantry Medal of the Navy, and a third proved to be the Black Eagle of Germany. I had a book giving all the ribbons of Europe, and as soon as anything was produced I was able to see whether it was the ribbon of any existing medal or decoration. Kitchener became quite exasperated and said: 'This damned fellow contradicts me whenever I say anything. We'll have no nonsense; I've got it, plain black and white, simple and dignified,' to which I remarked that that happened to be the Iron Cross. That broke up the meeting, and Kitchener said he would choose the ribbon with the King.

"The King and Kitchener spent half an hour choosing medal ribbons. I left a book containing all British ribbons and one with all foreign ones on the table, with a basket containing all the different coloured ribbons which my wife got for me. I put in a prominent place the card with my wife's suggestions, so that they might see what possibilities there were. Eventually I was sent for and shown with triumph a ribbon they had selected which was not in any book; I found they had chosen the one my wife had made out, mauve on a white ground. Certainly this was very distinctive, and not likely to be mistaken for any existing decoration.

"It was decided to call the new medal the Military Cross, but there was no guarantee that it would not be given for services at the base or on the line of communication, which was a great pity. The King then proposed to start a Military Medal."

And so the dreadful business of awarding class-orientated decorations went on, for the Military Medal was to be the non-commissioned officers' and privates' equivalent of the Military Cross. Crosses for officers, medals for men was to be a pattern slavishly echoed by the other branches of the armed forces, the Navy having its Distinguished Service Cross and Distinguished Service Medal, the Air Force its Distinguished Flying Cross and Distinguished Flying Medal. As for Sir Frederick's dislike of the idea of awarding the Military Cross to staff officers, its most distinguished non-combatant recipient, although greatly against his will, was in the end the Prince of Wales.

There remains one last honour, bestowed on a large number of people entirely by virtue of their office, and upon a few others as a reward for party political services. This is membership of Her Majesty's Most Honourable Privy Council. The archbishops of Canterbury and York and the bishop of London are automatically sworn on appointment, and like all privy councillors they retain their membership for life. Every member of the cabinet is also automatically a member, together with the leaders of the main opposition parties in Parliament, although this is a fairly recent innovation; an official leader of the opposition was only formally recognized in 1937. In 1924, Ramsay MacDonald, who had never before held cabinet office, had to be admitted to the Privy Council by George V before he was able to kiss hands as prime minister. Few members ever attend a meeting of the council, and when they do they stand throughout (so does the monarch), sometimes having spent many tedious hours travelling to Balmoral for the privilege. The original purpose of privy councillors before the evolution of cabinet government was to advise the sovereign, and quite literally to be privy to state secrets, and to some extent these functions still pertain. As a member of the Privy Council, a Member of Parliament may well be entrusted with information he or she would not otherwise have been able to obtain, and privy councillors are frequently chosen to head enquiries or commissions. A privy councillor who were to bring his or her own reputation into disrepute, or be convicted of a serious offence (although charges of drunken driving do not seem to count), would be expected to resign, but not necessarily compelled. Tainted by scandal, Jeremy Thorpe retained his membership; having lied to the House of Commons, John Profumo relinquished his. In 1976, after being convicted of fraud, John Stonehouse was expelled.

The Queen personally appoints to her Privy Council members of the Royal Family and Household (the Duke of Edinburgh and the Prince of Wales are both members; so is the Queen's private secretary), but appointments which appear in the honours lists are generally those recommended by the prime minister. George V, however, insisted on membership of the Privy Council for his doctor, Lord Dawson of Penn, against the wishes of his prime minister. Another appointment for which the king was responsible, unusual because in the circumstances so relatively demeaning, was that of Prince Louis of Battenberg, created Marquess of Milford Haven after being forced to resign as First Sea Lord in 1914. Privy Councillors are styled the Right Honourable. Because many peers who are not privy councillors also call themselves the Right Honourable (probably incorrectly), peers who are privy councillors sometimes also place PC after their name. It fell to George V in 1929 to accept, and welcome, the first woman privy councillor, Miss Margaret Bondfield, appointed that year as Minister of Labour with a seat in the cabinet. While the new Labour ministers were being sworn in at Windsor Castle, the king broke with tradition by speaking. He told Miss Bondfield how pleased he was to receive her, and "his smile as he spoke," she later recorded, "was cordial and sincere".

CHAPTER FIVE

"A Sorry Ambition"

The voracity of these things quite surprises me. I wonder people do not begin to feel the distinction of an unadorned name.

Sir Robert Peel.

George I shared with James I an almost total ignorance of the country he inherited, and one consequence was the ability of ministers to wrest from him the right to nominate appointments to the Order of the Garter, on the grounds that the king knew nothing of the life and worth of his subjects. Yet the Hanoverians continued to rule, not just to reign, and they exercised political patronage on a scale commensurate with their very considerable political influence. Over a century after the accession of George I, his great-great-grandson, William IV, still retained the power to dismiss a ministry, and in 1832 he would cheerfully have anticipated the events of seventy-nine years later by swamping the House of Lords with compliant peers had the Upper House failed to pass the great Reform Bill. Real power during the reigns of certainly the first three Hanoverians still resided with those who controlled the country's finances — the king and his First Lord of the Treasury, the forerunner of our prime minister — and by the time of George III the House of Lords was in practice little more than a tool of the king. Honours remained almost entirely political in origin.

The Honours System

In 1783 George III instituted the Most Illustrious Order of St Patrick, restricted to fifteen members (later raised to twenty-five), and in 1815 George IV extended the Order of the Bath to admit companions, but there was no enthusiasm for enfranchising within the honours system anyone who might not have expected a peerage or a knighthood in medieval times. Sir Robert Peel, who tended, like Lord Liverpool, to hold the whole business of honours at arm's length and to recommend only those he thought had rendered outstanding service to the nation, supported the continued distribution of awards like the Bath to naval and military officers, but he fervently hoped no order of chivalry would ever be instituted for men in civil life. "I cannot think," he told the House of Commons in 1834, "that it would raise the character of science in this country to establish a new system of reward and I deprecate the institution of a new order for them. In my opinion, it really would have conferred little additional credit on Sir Isaac Newton [a knight bachelor] if that eminent man had appeared with a blue ribbon, a red ribbon or a Star upon his chest. The practice would not be correspondent with the simplicity of the English character. I see a clear distinction between military service and scientific merit."

It was not until the middle years of Queen Victoria's reign that the outline of a constitutional monarchy began to take definite shape, with the sovereign's prerogatives in the matter of honours gradually slipping out of her hands and into those of party politicians. Once the queen became obliged to call upon the government's choice of party leader, and even to accept a prime minister she found anathema, there became little she could do but accept their recommendations for the majority of honours — instituting at the same time one or two of her own: the Most Exulted Order of the Star of India in 1861, the Royal Victoria and Albert in 1862, the Most Eminent Order of the Indian Empire and the Imperial Order of the Crown of India, both in 1877, and the Royal Victorian Order in 1896. She even toyed with the idea of an order exclusively for Welshmen, to be called the Order of St David had it been instituted.

"A Sorry Ambition"

In the matter of the peerage, however, Queen Victoria did manage to exercise her habitual quirkiness from time to time, on one occasion suffering a humiliating rebuff as a result. In 1856 she gave a judge, Sir James Parke, a life peerage (thus anticipating by twenty years the Appellate Jurisdiction Act of 1876), with the title Lord Wensleydale, but the Committee of Privileges considered this life peerage contrary to usage, to the principles of the constitution and the privileges of Parliament, and ruled that his letters patent did not entitle him to sit in the House of Lords. She had better luck creating peeresses in their own right. Lady Ottoline Morrell's mother, Mrs Arthur Bentinck, missed becoming Duchess of Portland through the premature death of her husband, which meant that unless something special was done for her, she would remain Mrs Bentinck when her children were eventually accorded, as is usual practice, the dignity and titles that would have been theirs had their father lived to inherit a peerage. So the queen compensated her with the title Baroness Bolsover. When Disraeli left office in 1868 he was persuaded to remain in the Commons, a prospect that seemed likely to preclude his wife from one day sharing in the honours of an earldom, for she was twelve years his senior and already ill. He asked the queen to bestow a title on her, choosing Viscountess Beaconsfield, and this the queen was graciously pleased to do, expressing to her adored Dizzy "her deep sense of Mr Disraeli's kindness and consideration towards her, not only in what concerned her personally, but in listening to her wishes". She was rewarded with a letter that began: "Mr Disraeli, at your Majesty's feet...." A more recent instance of a woman being raised to the peerage after the death of her husband occurred in 1943 when the widow of the Speaker of the House of Commons, Mrs Fitz-Roy, was created Viscountess Daventry on the grounds that her husband would have received a viscountcy on his retirement had he lived.

It is hardly surprising that the hallmark of Queen Victoria's reign, the industrial revolution, should have left its mark on the honours system. In 1885 the vote was given to agricultural workers, thus lessening the influence of the county aristocracy, and as England ceased to be an agricultural society and turned increasingly for its wealth to manufacturing industry, it was cash that counted, not land. A new peer in Victoria's time, other than a minister, was expected to have an income of at least £5,000 (and a baronet £2,000), but this was hardly a hurdle on the road to the House of Lords for men like Sir Arthur Guinness, the first brewer to be ennobled — by Disraeli. He baulked at calling himself Lord Guinness and chose instead the barely pronounceable name of Lord Ardilaun. In 1892 Sir Robert Peel must have turned in his grave when Lord Salisbury sent a scientist, Lord Kelvin, to the Upper House, followed three years later by the first of many newspaper proprietors, Lord Glenesk of the *Morning Post*, ennobled for "various villainies" according to the venomous but not always unreliable poet Alfred Douglas. Perhaps Gladstone's most popular recommendation for a peerage was Alfred Tennyson. Gladstone wrote 4,460 letters to Queen Victoria, and it is said that no fewer than 1,000 were concerned with honours.

Two characteristic attributes of Queen Victoria's times, prudery and propriety, certainly seem to have been holding sway in 1869, when the queen refused a British peerage for Baron Lionel Rothschild because, she wrote, he had made his money by "a species of gambling . . . far removed from the legitimate trading wh. she *delights to honour,* in which men have raised themselves by patient industry & unswerving probity to positions of wealth and influence". "Unswerving probity" was demanded in private conduct, too, at any rate so far as marriage was concerned. No divorcee was created a peer until in 1921 George V, most reluctantly, ennobled Sir George Riddell — appropriately enough the chairman of the company that owned the *News of the World*. But towards the end of the century, the Liberals, traditionally far less well off than the Tories, began to feel the pinch, to such an extent that the shades of James and Buckingham were called up to come to the aid of the party. In her *Memories of Fifty Years,* published in 1909, Lady St Helier claimed that the Bishop of Peterborough, Dr Magee, had been offered £50,000 for diocesan funds if he

"A Sorry Ambition"

were to secure a baronetcy for the donor; and Lord Suffield, eventually a Lord-in-Waiting-in-Ordinary to George V, recalled being offered the prospect of a sea-wall round his estate at Cromer if he would use his influence at court to procure a peerage, and even, by someone else, £250,000 for a title.[1]

It was extension of the franchise coupled with a redistribution of parliamentary seats that stretched Liberal Party funds so badly; £40,000 a year was considered adequate in 1880, but by 1895 nearer double that figure was needed. The expense of running party headquarters grew from £10,000 a year in the 1860s to around £100,000 a year by 1912. The temptation, if not actually to sell honours then at least to hold them out as a bribe for services rendered, became increasingly difficult to resist. With a baronetcy in mind, the Tory leader in the Commons wrote in 1880 to a fellow Conservative faced with the prospect of fighting a difficult seat: "I know that I am asking a great deal from you; but I trust you will be willing to make the sacrifice; & it will be felt a great addition to the claims you already have upon the gratitude of the Conservative party." The traffic was of course two-way, but not always successfully engineered. In 1891 the Tory MP for the Wisbech division of Cambridgeshire threatened to resign his seat unless he was given a baronetcy, and had his bluff called by the party managers. Others, too, were disappointed by Lord Salisbury, who had declared in 1885, when forming his first administration, that the experience of being importuned for honours had been a revelation to him "of the baser side of human nature". Even Sir George Elliot, who had spent over £120,000 on electioneering, was refused the peerage he coveted.

The approach for titles was often refreshingly blatant. One semi-literate member of Parliament wrote to Salisbury's chief whip in 1891: "Judging from The Times's political articles, & from what one hears on every side, the coming General Election will probably be anything but a quiet walkover for the Conservatives. It appears therefore that it wd. hardly be politic

1. *My Memories: 1830-1913.*

to look coldly on any offers of assistance, be they personal or otherwise, that may be made. As I have before stated, I am wishful to be created a Baronet, & tho' to persons placed in the high position occupied by Lord Salisbury this may seem to be but a sorry ambition, still to me it wd. be an advance in the social scale, & one wh. I am prepared to make sacrifices to obtain.

"Personally I feel I am unfitted for Parliamentary life, as I have not the power to express myself either concisely or with any fluency — but tho' I know I sd. be but of little use to my Party in this respect, still I could probably do good service in other ways — either by assisting suitable & clever candidates, who otherwise wd. be unable to stand the expenses of a contested election, & whose services wd. thus be lost to the Conservative party — or else by subscribing to some Political Fund, wh. indirectly wd. be of use to the cause."

He was told there was nothing doing until whose who had "long laboured for the party & bled for it" had been considered, and the poor man had to wait fourteen years for his advance in the social scale.

Three years on, in May 1894, sufficient unease about the disposition of honours was felt for the House of Commons to hold a light-hearted debate on the subject, when Sir William Lawson and Mr George Lambert proposed, unsuccessfully, that nominations for honours should be accompanied by a statement from the queen outlining the services said to have been rendered, a statement similar to the citation published when an award was made of the Victoria Cross.

Something of a minor political scandal was to come to a head the following year, with its roots in the general elections of 1885 and 1886. These two contests, fought so close together, had left the Liberal Party so desperately short of funds that the party's chief whip, Arnold Morley, and the chief Liberal organizer, Francis Schnadhorst, sounded out a banker, Sydney Stern, and a new member of the Commons, James Williamson, MP for Lancaster, to see if they fancied buying a peerage. Negotiations dragged on to the point where Lord Rosebery was left holding the baby. Feeling that promises made by a previous administration should be honoured, he allowed Mr Stern and Mr Williamson (the latter, in the event, did not even trouble to take his seat in the House of Lords for two years) to appear in the July 1895 resignation honours list, and they became Lord Wandsworth and Lord Ashton. But he let it be known in the *Daily News* that they were in effect Gladstone's nominees. In its most sarcastic eighteenth-century vein, the *Spectator* commented on the affair, "There is no allegation that either Mr Stern or Mr Williamson have ever done anything worthy of reward but supply the party war chest."

But this was to prove only a dress-rehersal for the major political scandal that blew up that year, over a baronetcy, and for all Lord Rosebery's attempts to deflect criticism of the two new peers on to Gladstone, it blew up in his own face. For in his list appeared the name of a young man of 31, Captain Herbert Naylor-Leyland, of whom only a handful of constituents and fellow members of Parliament would ever have heard had not the gallant captain resigned his seat early in 1895, a seat he had won three years before for the Conservatives, announcing one of the most spectacular and instantaneous conversions of all time, in his case to the cause of Liberalism. The immediate result of his action was to enable the Liberal candidate, Sir Weetman Pearson, later Lord Cowdray, to enter Parliament. This occurred on 19 February. On 1 July, Captain Naylor-Leyland was Sir Herbert.

In accordance with normal practice, *The Times* was in possession of an embargoed copy of the honours list, and was able to thunder on the day Naylor-Leyland's ill-gotten baronetcy was announced:

"Captain Naylor-Leyland never did anything of which the public heard until he suddenly deserted the Unionist party, and by quitting his seat in Colchester at an inconvenient moment deliberately threw the reputation of that borough into the hands of his Radical opponent. He has now undertaken to oppose Mr Curzon, one of the members of the Government, at Southport. Considering that down to the day when he resigned his seat for Colchester, a few months ago, Captain

Naylor-Leyland had never given any hint in public that the avowed opinions on which he had been elected had been changed, it is not too much to say that such an apostasy, whatever regard it may deserve who profit by it, ought not to be singled out for honour by the responsible advisors of the Queen."

Sir Herbert Naylor-Leyland failed to win Southport, perhaps because he had the stuffing completely knocked out of him by a second, even more blistering, broadside launched by Henry Labouchere in the radical organ *Truth*.

"There is one Liberal defeat for which I shall not weep," wrote Labouchere. "It is that of Sir H. Naylor-Leyland, who is fighting for the seat of Mr G. Curzon. His baronetcy becomes more mysterious every day. If Lord Rosebery denies that he is responsible for it — who is? Apparently we are expected to believe that the Queen had a happy thought, and when the list of honours was submitted to her by the late Premier, said, 'There is one man whose name, to my surprise, is not on the list. Why is not that noble, that pure, patriotic, that stern and unbending politician, Captain Naylor-Leyland, not given a Baronetcy? I insist that he shall at least have one, although, in my opinion, he is as much entitled to a Peerage as the eloquent Stern, and the statesmanlike Williamson!' I do not hesitate to say that whoever was concerned in granting this 'honour' to Captain Naylor-Leyland is as much disgraced by it as the Captain is in accepting it. I estimate that this Baronetcy and the peerages of Messrs Stern and Williamson will cost the Party more seats than the money that they may have brought into the Parliamentary chest will do good. 'It does not smell,' said Vespasian of the money that he acquired from a tax on the latrines in Rome. But the money brought in by this trafficking in hereditary legislatorships reeks of corruption. It stinks!"

Those men who had "raised themselves by patient industry and unswerving propity" only made gradual inroads into the House of Lords during Queen Victoria's reign, no matter how much the queen may have claimed that she delighted to honour them. Between 1876 and 1884 only four industrialists were ennobled, and it took another decade for a further eighteen commercial or industrial peerages to be created, although by 1896 a quarter of all the peers held directorships, and by the turn of the century five square miles of inner London were owned by just nine families, most notably those of the dukes of Bedford, Portland and Westminster. During roughly the same period, a total of about a hundred new peers were created. For all their occasional betrayal of "traditional" Victorian values, Queen Victoria's prime ministers were amazingly frugal in their recommendations for peerages when compared to those who came after the two world wars. In the twenty years between 1875 and 1894, 110 new peers were made, an average of 5.5 a year; during the two decades between 1925 and 1944, the number almost doubled, to 207. It rose even more spectacularly in the decade immediately after the Second World War, when 135 new peers were created. The overall effect of these new creations, taking into account those peerages that fell into abeyance during the same period, or became extinct, was to increase the peerage of the realm from 400 members at the start of Victoria's reign to 916 by 1962. The heyday of the baronets arrived under Edward VII's and George V's premiers. Between 1905 and 1934, no fewer than 649 baronetcies were gazetted, many of them for industrialists and many of them purchased for party funds; by contrast, the years 1945-54 saw only 51. It was, however, the new knights who marched ever onwards and upwards. Between 1875 and 1884, Queen Victoria dubbed 448 men; between 1905 and 1954, 10,503 gentlemen, not all of them precisely in the mould of Sir Launcelot, knelt before their sovereign. Commenting contemporaneously on Edwardian England, the American writer A. L. Lowell quite simply noted: "Respect for the old territorial aristocracy has been replaced by a veneration for titles."

While titles may in themselves have been venerated, and greatly sought after for their own sake, at stake too was the peaceful development of democratic government, for the House of Lords continued to maintain a huge built-in Conservative majority, able to frustrate at will any legislation enacted by a Liberal government. The seeds of the constitutional crisis that eventually confronted George V the moment he came to the throne had been sown in his grandmother's time, when a mass defection of Liberal peers resulted, in 1893, in the rejection by the Lords of Home Rule for Ireland, by 419 votes to 41. The ultimate imbalance in the majorities between the two Houses of Parliament was arrived at in 1906 when the Liberals were returned to power with an overall majority in the Commons of 356, to be confronted by a House of Lords containing a majority of almost 400 Conservatives. The assault by the House of Lords upon the Education Bill of 1906 and the Licensing Bill of 1908 were only two examples of their power to undo the work of the elected Commons that prompted Lloyd George to coin his memorable and ever since much plagiarized assertion that the House of Lords, far from being the watchdog of the constitution, was Mr Balfour's poodle.

Death alone was to save King Edward VII from having to face up to and cope with a monumental crisis affecting the honours system which had been brewing, in practical terms, for perhaps a hundred years, and in essence lay in the centuries-old conflict between the rights of an elected Commons versus those of a hereditary peerage. Lloyd George's detestation of the Upper House rankled with Edward VII when in 1906 the Welsh firebrand made "another indecent attack on the House of Lords", as the king's private secretary complained to the prime minister. The Palace pointed out that Lloyd George was anxious for the king and queen to go to Cardiff to open new docks, but that nothing would induce the king to visit Cardiff "unless Mr Lloyd George learns how to behave with propriety as a Cabinet Minister holding an important Office". In 1909 Lloyd George, by then Chancellor of the Exchequer, returned to his attack on the House of Lords, complaining that a fully equipped duke was as costly to maintain as two dreadnoughts, and less easy to scrap. It was the year in which he introduced a highly controversial budget, ostensibly to pay for pensions and the naval arms race, and so fiercely did the Conservatives oppose it in the Commons that 544 division bells rang before the Lords got a chance to look at

"A Sorry Ambition"

it. When they did, they threw it out by 350 votes to 75, the first time a finance Bill had been rejected by the Upper House since the seventeenth century. Notwithstanding King Edward's assessment of Lloyd George's politics as "socialism of the most insidious kind" he was equally appalled by the House of Lords' threats to reject the budget, telling one of his private secretaries, Lord Knollys, that he thought the peers were mad. With no money with which to govern, the prime minister called a general election, fought, inevitably, on the question who was to govern, the Commons or the Lords. The Liberals retained their overall majority and the Lords passed the Finance Bill. The crisis seemed to be over.

But Herbert Asquith, the Liberal prime minister, thought he now saw his opportunity to curtail drastically the legislative powers of the House of Lords, and he proposed that they should no longer have the right to amend or reject a money Bill, or to delay other legislation beyond twenty-five months. The problem would be in persuading the Lords to agree to legislation curbing their own powers. The solution seemed very neat if rather distasteful; to invite the king to squander his prerogative as the fountain of honour by creating enough peers, exclusively for party political purposes, to swamp the Conservative majority in the House of Lords, no matter how ludicrous such a spectacle of instantly ennobled barons might appear to the electorate. King Edward's sudden death on 6 May 1910 landed this unpalatable plan in the lap of his son.

Having an elder brother, George V — like Henry VIII and Charles I — had not originally expected to succeed to the throne. He was inexperienced, shy, nervous and genuinely bereaved by the death of his father, and Asquith very properly did his best to avoid an immediate general election by agreeing to party talks on the future of the House of Lords. But within three weeks of his accession, the king was fussing about the possibility of peerages being recommended in the Birthday Honours List. In fact, he asked that there should be none, "as during the transitional state of the House of Lords he would be reluctant to agree to them". Asquith protested, and Lord Knollys wrote to say, "The King yields reluctantly and hopes that only a limited number of names, carefully selected, will be submitted to him." Asquith and Balfour, leader of the opposition, began their discussions on Lords reform on 17 June, and within twenty-four hours the prime minister received a prompting note from Knollys. "The King hopes that the question of Life Peers may if possible be brought before the conference," he wrote. "He is strongly in favour of them as I believe are most sensible people." But nothing came of that idea for another forty-eight years, and by November the talks had broken down. On 11 November the king received the prime minister at York Cottage, the poky little house on the Sandringham estate where he liked to live in domestic claustrophobia, and noted afterwards in his flat and homely diary: "At 6.30 the Prime Minister arrived. Had two long talks with him. He reported that the Conference had failed and he proposes to dissolve and have a general election and get it over before Xmas. He asked me for *no guarantees*." The king's underlining of those two words were echoed in the record kept by his second private secretary, Sir Arthur Bigge, who noted, "He did not ask for anything from the King; *no promises, no guarantees during this Parliament*."

The fear all along had been that the prime minister would ask the king to guarantee the creation of new peers should the need arise. Under the constitution, only the sovereign can create a peer; his possible refusal to accede to a recommendation made by the prime minister is another matter, and part of the constitutional crisis now unfolding was the danger that the king and his prime minister might be brought into direct confrontation should Asquith request new peers and George V, in what he took to be unseemly circumstances likely to bring the House of Lords and the entire honours system into ridicule, refuse them.

And indeed, three days later the king's fears were proved to be far from groundless and his relief short-lived, for Asquith went back on the undertaking he had left with the king, drafting a cabinet minute advising the king to grant an immediate dissolution of Parliament, which contained the following provisory clause: "His Majesty's Ministers cannot, however, take the responsibility of advising dissolution, unless they may understand that, in the event of the policy of the Government being approved by an adequate majority in the new House of Commons, His Majesty will be ready to exercise his constitutional powers (which may involve the Prerogative of creating peers), if needed, to secure that effect should be given to the decision of the country."

This note was a double volte-face, for in February the previous year Asquith had told the House of Commons: "To ask in advance for a blank authority for an indefinite exercise of the Royal Prerogative in regard to a measure which had never been submitted to, or approved by, the House of Commons, is a request which, in my judgement, no constitutional statesman can properly make and is a concession which the Sovereign cannot be expected to grant." George V may well have wondered why it was that his father had not been expected to make such a grant, and suddenly he was.

The truth is, at the end of the day the sovereign is as fully obliged to create peers at the government's request as he is to abdicate should Parliament place the necessary document on his desk. What George V objected to was being asked for promises before the matter had been settled at a general election, as though he could not be trusted to understand and carry out his constitutional duties when the crunch came. Lord Knollys, a partisan of the Asquith administration, advised the king to indicate to the prime minister his willingness to create new peers should the Lords decline to sanction a reduction in their powers, and what resulted, as we learn from the king's diary entry for 16 November 1910, was that after a long talk with Asquith and Lord Crewe, Leader of the House of Lords, the king agreed "most reluctantly to give the Cabinet a secret understanding that in the event of the Government being returned with a majority at the General Election, I should use my Prerogative to make Peers if asked for. [It is amusing in this context to note that two words the king had difficulty spelling were "perrogative" and "scandel".] I disliked having to do this very much, but agreed that this was the only alternative to the

The Honours System

Cabinet resigning, which at this moment would be disastrous." The king told his friend Lord Derby that Asquith and Crewe had put a pistol to his head, bullied him for an hour, forbidden him to see the leaders of the opposition and refused to make public the pledge. In agreeing to Asquith's demands for secret guarantees, the king eventually followed the advice of one of his joint private secretaries, Lord Knollys, while rejecting the fundamentally opposed views of Knollys's colleague, Sir Arthur Bigge. "Francis strongly urged me to take this course," the king wrote, "and I think his advice is generally very sound. I only trust and pray he is right this time." The king's assistant private secretary, Sir Frederick Ponsonby, was "horrified" when he first learned what had happened.[2]

As Kenneth Rose has written in his life of George V,[3] "The episode of contingent guarantees left the King with a lifelong grievance. He resented not so much the supposed strain put on the constitution by the Cabinet's demands; that was a matter for interpretation on which two such experienced public servants as Knollys and Bigge would take contrary views. What rankled in the King's mind was the indignity of having been browbeaten and bullied, of not having been trusted to do his duty when the time came. Above all, he was shocked by Asquith's insistence that his pledge should remain secret." In the event, the Liberals increased their majority in the Commons; the 1911 Parliament Act, which abolished the power of the Lords to amend or reject a money Bill, and ensured that a Bill passed in three successive sessions by the Commons would automatically become law, was accepted by the House of Lords when the king's secret promise became public knowledge and they realized the alternative to giving way was to be swamped by Liberal peers; and the king was never called upon to redeem his pledge. None of this happened, however, before Asquith had earned himself an entry in the *Oxford Dictionary of Quotations*: "We had better wait and see." It was a phrase he used repeatedly in 1910,

2. *Recollections of Three Reigns.*
3. *King George V* (London, Weidenfeld & Nicolson, 1983).

"A Sorry Ambition"

while waiting upon events of his own invention.

A way to circumvent any further interference by the House of Lords in financial affairs was to be dreamed up at the Labour Party Conference at Hastings in October 1933, when Sir Stafford Cripps called on the next Labour government to abolish the House of Lords and then to pass an Emergency Powers Act which would "take over and regulate the financial machine". Meanwhile, the king reserved the right to sound huffy when Asquith submitted names of potential peers for the Coronation Honours List. "[The King's] own strong impression is that to create Peers under existing circumstances and until the crisis is over would be a mistake and a mockery," Lord Knollys began a letter to Asquith, "especially in view of the possible or probable creation of 500 Peers." The king's figure of 500 seems only to have been mildly exaggerated; without waiting for the ultimate necessity, Asquith had drawn up a provisional list of 245 names to whom he intended offering the Liberal whip in the House of Lords. They included backbenchers, heirs to peerages, financiers, soldiers, a composer, a chemist, a surgeon, an engineer, Thomas Hardy, Bertrand Russell (who was not to inherit his earldom until 1931), Gilbert Murray, James Barrie, the millionaire tea-merchant Sir Thomas Lipton, who had almost certainly been nominated for his knighthood by Queen Alexandra when she was Princess of Wales (he had covered the deficit incurred by the Princess's plan to hold a dinner for London's poor as part of Queen Victoria's Diamond Jubilee celebrations in 1897), Joseph Rowntree, Winston Churchill's brother John and Sir George Lewis, a solicitor who specialized in the seamy side of litigation (as lawyer to Lady Charles Beresford, he had even been involved in one of Edward VII's indiscreet sexual imbroglios). Writing to Lord Stamfordham six days after the crucial vote, when the Parliament Bill was passed by 17 votes, the king had this to say: "I am afraid it is impossible to pat the Opposition on the back, but I am indeed grateful for what they have done & saved me from a humiliation from which I should never have survived. If the creation had taken place, I should never have been the same person again." And in his letter to

The Honours System

Asquith on the subject of the Coronation Honours List, Lord Knollys went on: "The King says he does not pretend to understand the logic of these people who while vilifying the House of Lords on every convenient occasion are yet apparently anxious to become members of that Body."

Among the names which eventually appeared in the honours list and cannot have thrilled the king were a brother-in-law of the prime minister, down for a barony, and advancement for Lord Crewe, one of the men who had so recently browbeaten and bullied him, from earl to marquess. While compiling the list Asquith told Balfour, surely not with a great deal of conviction, that it was a task "as you well know, as uncongenial and even hateful as can befall a man". He later accepted an earldom. The king's task in approving the list seems to have been little less congenial than Asquith's in submitting it, and one earl, Lord Aberdeen, appeared to the king so unsuitable for promotion to marquess "in view of his incompetency and of his being the laughing stock of everybody who has to do with him" that he had to wait another five years to become Marquess of Aberdeen & Temair.

During his reign, George V had many burdens to bear, not the least heavy of which was the honours system. Those who sought to manipulate it, and him, seldom seem to have left him in peace. Lloyd George was forever promising honours to the recipients before informing the king, who would then at least have had the opportunity of exercising two of his most important constitutional functions, of offering advice and warning. Without enjoyment of the third of his vital constitutional prerogatives, the right to be kept informed, he was denied any chance of exercising the other two, and thus, in the case of honours, of having an opportunity of protesting at some of the names put forward. Within six months of giving the Canadian mountebank Max Aitken a baronetcy, Lloyd George told him he could have a peerage, and he became Lord Beaverbrook, but not before the king had expressed, through Lord Stamfordham (formally Sir Arthur Bigge; the king honoured him with a peerage at the Coronation), his surprise and hurt. "His Majesty commands me," Stamfordham wrote,

"A Sorry Ambition"

in language icily formal coming from a private secretary to a prime minister, "to say that he feels that the Sovereign's Prerogatives in this respect should not be disregarded, and he trusts that in future no honours whatever will be offered to any Minister until his approval has been informally obtained." With studied arrogance Lloyd George ignored Stamfordham's letter, so the king returned to the offensive by instructing Stamfordham to send Lloyd George a formal memorandum, reminding him the Crown was the fountain of honour, that honours could only be conferred by the king, acting on the advice of his ministers, and it was therefore only right that the king should be informally consulted before an honour was promised or divulged. Still Lloyd George declined to consent in writing to the king's requests, for he had every intention of repeating his offence — by promising the incompetent minister in charge of the newly constituted Air Force, Lord Rothermere, that he might have a viscountcy on his retirement. This drew from Buckingham Palace the information that the king gave his approval "but with much reluctance", for it was "another case of a quasi promise, and what is worse, a quasi committal of His Majesty!"

Forever trying to tug back some semblance of control over the distribution of honours, the king was always touched and pleased when anyone actually recognized that their honour did emanate from himself, not from 10 Downing Street. The first prime minister of Northern Ireland, Sir James Craig, wrote to the king to thank him for his viscountcy, and was told by Lord Stamfordham, "I know [your letter] will be appreciated by His Majesty, as *nowadays* such expressions of thanks to the Sovereign are the exception rather than the rule." Another grateful recipient of the royal bounty who sent his personal thanks was Sir Edward Elgar. In 1931, already garlanded with honours, he received a baronetcy, and wrote to Sir Frederick Ponsonby to say: "I do not know if it is permissible to send personal thanks to His Majesty the King; but if it is allowed, I shall be grateful to you if you find it possible to convey to His Majesty an expression of my sincere thanks for the honour that I am informed by the Prime

Minister is to be bestowed on me." Elgar had particularly good cause to feel indebted to the king, having already received two honours in his personal gift, the Order of Merit and the KCVO. Perhaps it was Elgar's letter of thanks for the baronetcy that prompted George V, two years later, to advance him to GCVO.

It was George V's mercurial Welsh prime minister Lloyd George whose conduct was to lay the greatest burden in the matter of honours on the shoulders of his conscientious monarch. "You and I know that the sale of honours is the cleanest way of raising money for a political party," Lloyd George is said to have told Lord Davidson. "The worst of it is you cannot defend it in public." What Lloyd George seems to have been implying is that to attack the sale of honours is a form of hypocrisy, and it is certainly true that as the scrutiny of public life has become easier through the telescope provided by the press and television, so our demands that public men and women should behave like the angels we are not has grown louder. It is true too that in hawking political honours, Lloyd George was following a habit pursued in the past by kings. But even in the seventeenth century it was a habit frowned upon and satirized, for it was seen not only to bring cash into needy coffers but dishonour upon honour, and to serve as an affront and positive danger to the very establishment the peerage existed to protect. The best that can be said for Lloyd George was that in selling honours with a reckless disregard for prudence he overreached himself; certainly his resulting fall was accompanied by a clatter commensurate with his contempt for the dignity of the Crown, and his own arrogant, egotistical, intemperate nature.

In just eighteen months, between January 1921 and June 1922, Lloyd George sold seventy-four baronetcies, but any temptation to lampoon the prime minister has always to be balanced by a measure of criticism of those pathetic parvenus who wished to enhance their standing in the community by the purchase of a title, for which in the reign of George V there was a going rate: £100,000 for a peerage, £40,000 for a baronetcy, £10,000 for a knighthood. Many of the baronetcies were

"A Sorry Ambition"

offered in London clubs by Sir William Sutherland, whom everyone cordially loathed and Lloyd George had the temerity to foist on George V as Chancellor of the Duchy of Lancaster. But the most spectacular purveyor of titles, a kind of broker in peerages, was the notorious crook, man about town and entrepreneur, Maundy Gregory, a man who came to be associated indelibly with the twentieth-century sale of honours, and whose nefarious activities were to result in the establishment of a political honours scrutiny committee and an Act of Parliament, under which he himself was eventually prosecuted.

CHAPTER SIX
Maundy Gregory

History has yet to reveal — perhaps it never will fully reveal — the measure of corruption which Lloyd George permitted to enter politics during his six years as Prime Minister.

Lord Blake.

Arthur John Peter Michael Maundy Gregory, born in Southampton in 1877, was the son of an Anglo-Catholic parish priest and a mother whom, it was alleged, Maundy Gregory (or J. Maundy-Gregory, as he liked to be known throughout most of his esoteric and lucrative career) permitted to die in an almshouse. He had an office at 38 Parliament Street, conveniently close to the Houses of Parliament for the benefit of whose members he ran a brokerage. It was not, however, in stocks and shares that he dealt, but in the sale for party profit of baronetcies and peerages. On a side table stood a signed photograph of the Duke of York, later King George VI, at whose wedding Gregory was a steward, receiving from the Duke a gold cigarette case, and in Maundy Gregory's breast pocket reposed a second gold cigarette case, a gift from King George II of Greece. Even odder, a portrait of Judge Jeffreys hung on the wall.

Maundy Gregory was very much a man of his time; had he not existed he would have been invented, most probably by Evelyn Waugh, who did in fact gain a reputation for embroidering fanciful tales of Gregory's exploits (the truth was far stranger than anything Waugh cooked up) for the entertainment of his dinner guests. Lloyd George needed money for party funds; men who had done well out of the war, by selling boots to the army or by supplying armaments (in the case of one manufacturer, no less than 75 million grenades), were desperate for social recognition; and Maundy Gregory himself possessed a fantasy life that required fulfilment. There were plenty of people around to help him attain it. They ranged from the brilliant but foolish Lord Birkenhead, whose friendship with Gregory was nothing short of idiotic, to an actress called Edith Rosse, with whom Gregory shared a house and to whom he was not averse to being thought to be married, although he was in fact homosexual. Sometimes he pretended that Mrs Rosse, who was separated from her husband Frederick Rosse, was his sister. That he later wrote out her will on the back of a hotel menu and was then suspected of her murder was merely part and parcel of a life style that makes it exceedingly difficult for public scandals in these puritanical days to live up to the very highest standards set in the sleazy past.

Maundy Gregory's prodigious energy and ambition might have served him well in any one of several callings (not inappropriately, his earliest dream was to go into the theatre), but his pretensions ideally suited him for the business of honours broker; he claimed descent from eight kings, including William the Conqueror. Harry Hotspur, John of Gaunt and the Black Prince were naturally three more royal ancestors whose very Englishness and glamour gave credence to his own unswerving loyalty to crown and empire. Another typical symptom of Maundy Gregory's unstable personality was his love of mystification, the need of a cloak-and-dagger existence, a way of carrying on that exhibits deep dissatisfaction with reality and a craving to be taken for someone else entirely. He told his friends that he was "principal co-organizer of the great secret anti-Bolshevik movement" and was in constant danger of being assassinated by Russian agents, which was why he required a taxi on permanent stand-by; the "taxi" was in fact his own car, painted, fitted up with a dummy meter and a peephole, and driven by his own chauffeur. It was no coincidence that one of his idols was the paranoid and probably half-mad writer Frederick Rolfe, whose notorious "Venetian letters" Gregory purchased for £150 from A.J.A. Symonds, author of *The Quest for Corvo*, a book in which Symonds recounts how Gregory called on him with a wad of notes amounting to £5,000; the need to handle cash in preference to transacting business with a cheque was another sign of Gregory's essential insecurity, as was his close identification with a man like Rolfe who laid claim to a spurious title, that of Baron Corvo.

Gregory's training in the sale of honours was undertaken by a couple of shady politicians, Alick Murray, Asquith's former chief whip, who briefly fled into exile in 1912 when it was discovered that without authority he had invested £9,000 in Marconi belonging to Liberal Party funds, and Freddy Guest, a dim-witted brother of Lord Wimborne and a cousin of Winston Churchill, whose contribution to the solving of social unrest in 1919 was to recommend that the workers be given beer. "The masses are hot and thirsty," he wrote to Lloyd George. "I believe a little 'dope' would keep them quiet." It was to this pair of nonentities that responsibility had been given by Lloyd George not just for selling honours but for putting the whole matter on a sound financial footing. Their solution was to squeeze out the reasonably well-intentioned wheelers and dealers and to place in position one key broker, someone without previous party allegiance and with apparently respectable credentials who could easily be ditched if things went wrong. Maundy Gregory was rabidly right-wing but happy to serve any paymaster. He was the son of a clergyman, he had been educated, although not very successfully, at a minor private school and at Oxford, and he was deemed to be eminently ditchable, for apart from the eccentric Rector of Stiffkey it is doubtful if he had a real friend in the world. He was, however, adept at laying on expensive dinners, at affecting a certain impressive style (he wore a scarab ring he claimed had belonged to Oscar Wilde), and at feigning indifference to wealth, one of the hallmarks of a genuinely wealthy man. They decided that J. Maundy-Gregory, former professional actor and in possession of a police record (he had once been fined £5 for allowing a 7-year-old girl to appear on the stage), was their man. Had they also known that he had tried his hand at blackmail it is doubtful even then whether they would have been deterred.

Gregory's office, supposedly the headquarters of the *Whitehall Gazette* and staffed by page-boys whose uniforms had been copied from those of government messengers, was of course a front. Such reassuring periodicals as the *Tatler* and *Country Life* lay around. The signed photographs (in addition to the Duke of York they included one of the Marshal of the Diplomatic Corps) were intended, along with all the paraphernalia on Gregory's desk (telephones, buzzers for secretaries and even phony red dispatch boxes), to convey his personal links with Downing Street and Buckingham Palace. To help entice into his web those "wishful to be created a Baronet" or anyone else desirous of an honour, Maundy Gregory just happened also to own a club, the Ambassador, where many of his potential clients lunched or dined, often at Gregory's expense. They were sometimes also introduced to Gregory by the managing director, a good-looking young man called Peter Mazzina whom Gregory had plucked from obscurity, at the age of 23, when he was a waiter at the Carlton Hotel, presenting him with a salary of £3,000 a year and the Noble Order of the Republic of San Marino. Those who accepted hospitality from Maundy Gregory at the Ambassador Club, not necessarily with immoral motives in mind, included such respectable Establishment figures as Winston Churchill and the Duke of Marlborough; indeed, the presence of men like these served as a convenient ruse to boost Gregory's own respectability. Once back in the offices of the *Whitehall Gazette,* those of Gregory's guests who were hoping that the club was a gateway to social preferment were confronted with the commercial facts of social life: a knighthood would cost them £10,000, a baronetcy £40,000 and a peerage £100,000. This was the kind of talk they and Gregory understood, and Lloyd George approved and encouraged. Maundy Gregory let it be known that he was forever popping in and out of Downing Street and Buckingham Palace, that a word in the right ear from himself could work wonders, and that a generous contribution to party funds would not go unrewarded. The Liberal Party's coffers were topped up, Gregory took his own very considerable cut, and the king not infrequently fretted and worried when improbable names appeared on honours lists submitted to him. Lloyd George, who never cared for monarchs or monarchy, gave George V one headache after another. Within two years of the Order of the British Empire being instituted, the order had been riddled with 22,000 members. The loyalty and lucre of an ex-convict who had traded with the enemy, of "guilty" parties in divorce proceedings and of no fewer than forty-nine newspaper proprietors, editors and managing directors were acquired by Lloyd George through the honours system.

Members of the old school began to find some of Lloyd George's nominees hard to swallow, men like Lieutenant-Colonel Henry Croft, MP, who complained in 1919 that "several of them would have been blackballed by any respectable London social club". Two years later the colonel had a specific case in mind when he rose to complain because a convicted food hoarder, Rowland Hodge, a man who had been on Maundy Gregory's list since 1912, had got a baronetcy "for public services". Hodge was a shipbuilder as well as a food hoarder, and he had been presented to George V in 1917 during a tour the king had made of the Tyneside shipyards. After the king had had Hodge's name thrust upon him for an honour, apparently without realizing he had been convicted in 1918, Lord Stamfordham wrote to Lloyd George's secretary: "The King . . . said he perfectly recollected the man as the only individual of a personally unattractive (to say the least of it) character whom he met on that tour." And he added, "The King has expressed to me his feelings of annoyance and indeed disgust that this man should have received any honour, yet alone a Baronetcy." Fortunately for the king, receipt by Hodge of a baronetcy as opposed to a knighthood did not entail the necessity of His Majesty meeting the man again, but it seems incredible that neither the king nor his private secretary had spotted the name of such a recently convicted criminal on the prime minister's honours list until too late. Lloyd George tried to bluff it out by admitting he knew that Hodge had a conviction but he deserved his baronetcy because he had "rendered conspicuous public services to the country during the war", but the *Morning Post* had the matter in more disinterested perspective when it questioned whether the delivery on time of ships he had been commissioned to build was "a service sufficient to extinguish conviction for food-hoarding of a particularly gross and flagrant kind". Among other items, Rowland Hodge was found to have in his house 1,148 lb of flour, 333⅓ lb of sugar, 148 lb 6 oz of bacon and ham, 29 lb of sago, 19½ lbs of split peas, 32 lb of lentils, 31 lb of rice, 25 tins of sardines, 10 jars of ox tongue, 19 tins of salmon, 85 lb of jam and marmalade and 61 tins of preserved fruits. He was fined £600. Lloyd George told Parliament the food had been hoarded without Hodge's knowledge.

Another recipient of Lloyd George's tainted gratitude who had covered himself in shame during the war was Sir William Vestey of the Union Cold Storage Company; having "rendered immense service" — in his case by shifting his meat-packing business to Buenos Aires in 1915 to avoid paying income tax, at the same time throwing 5,000 British out of work — Sir William was honoured by a barony in the 1922 Birthday Honours List. Once again the king professed ignorance of Sir William's activities. He certainly would not have known that two years before, Maundy Gregory had been paid £50,000 by a Dundee whisky distiller, Sir John Stewart, for a baronetcy "for public services". This was one purchased honour which in the end did Lloyd George no good; baronets are expected to be able to keep their end up, and when Sir John's financial position grew acute, the £50,000 was refunded. In 1924, with debts of £500,000, the luckless baronet shot himself. At his inquest, a solicitor representing one of the largest creditors publicly described Sir John as "a bootlegging pal of Mr Lloyd George".

The extent to which Lloyd George's trafficking in honours was common knowledge at the time was reflected by the song to which recruits still march while at ease, "Lloyd George knew my father, Father knew Lloyd George", sung to the tune of "Onward, Christian Soldiers" and first hummed *sotto voce* by aristocratic young men about town whenever one of the prime minister's parvenu baronets entered a London club. Indeed, so ridiculous did many of the recipients seem in the eyes of those who thought themselves morally superior that when Mr Hilberbrand Harmsworth, the younger brother of Lord Northcliffe and Lord Rothermere, acquired a baronetcy "for public services", his own family, well aware that he had never done a day's work in his life, inundated him with telegrams. "At last a grateful nation has given you your due reward," they read.

Among the hundreds of undeserved and unearned honours that were splattered about during the money-raising escapades of Lloyd George, his chief whips and his prime honours broker, Maundy Gregory, two that perhaps deserve pride of place concern the cases of Sir Joseph Robinson and Lord Farquhar. Farquhar's earldom was the more dramatic because it touched the king's honour even more closely than Robinson's barony, for Farquhar, who began life as the fifth son of a baronet, was a member of the royal household and a trusted personal friend of the king and queen.

Born in 1844, Farquhar had first been an intimate friend of Edward VII, and George V continued the relationship, addressing him as "My dear Horace" and signing his letters: "Your sincere old friend, G.R.I." Farquhar made a good deal of money through banking, gave a good deal of it to the Conservative Party, and in return received a baronetcy. After precisely three years in the House of Commons, as MP for West Marylebone, he went upstairs to the House of Lords, having explained, somewhat injudiciously, to one of Gladstone's secretaries that he had subscribed more than the "accepted tariff". Through his friendship with the Earl of Fife, created a duke on his marriage to King Edward's daughter Princess Louise, Farquhar gained access to royal circles, and was appointed Master of the Household, a privy councillor and an extra lord-in-waiting to King Edward. By way of gratitude he managed to inveigle several other members of the royal household in a financial scandal on the Stock Exchange, involving shares in a Siberian gold mine; the shares rocketed and then plummeted, leaving, it was said, Lord Farquhar £70,000 better off. Those who had lent their names to the venture included the king's private secretary.

On succeeding to the throne, George V appointed Farquhar a lord-in-waiting, and in 1915 Asquith made him Lord Steward of the Household (it was in those days a political appointment). In 1917, having got his valet exempted from military service, he was made a viscount. Both during and after the war, Farquhar spent money like water, and ended up with a house in Grosvenor Square, a lease on White Lodge in Richmond Park and a sub-lease from the king on Castle Rising in Norfolk. It was perhaps an additional stroke of good fortune which he scarcely deserved when at a dance at 7 Grosvenor Square the Duke of York and Lady Elizabeth Bowes-Lyon met for the first time in adult life, and when the future George VI and Queen Elizabeth married, Farquhar graciously lent them White Lodge for the first few months of their married life. In 1922, having been a viscount for only five years, Lord Farquhar received the Grand Cross of the Order of the Bath and an earldom. Few men of distinction have been so showered with honours, and it has to be remembered that Farquhar's chief claim to fame was as a lavish and generous host.

Whether Farquhar's honours went to his head, or his mind became a little unhinged on its own account, at all events he now became exceedingly eccentric, engaging in the most childish and obstreperous contretemps at court over matters of etiquette and precedence. He managed to antagonize both Lord Stamfordham and Sir Frederick Ponsonby, and when Lloyd George's government fell in 1922 not only were they delighted to be rid of a meddlesome Lord Steward but Lord Stamfordham insisted that it should be made plain that Farquhar's earldom had been created in recognition of political services, not for services to the court.

It may be that Stamfordham, through another of the king's friends, Lord Lincolnshire, had got wind of Farquhar's involvement in the sale of honours. "Horace Farquhar," Lincolnshire wrote, "who has a bad reputation in the City, is said to be the prime mover in this dirty business. Astor, who was made a viscount, paid £40,000 a year to the party funds through Horace till the day of his death." Farquhar had been treasurer of the Conservative Party, and in 1923 it began to transpire that he had been diverting funds donated to the party, and was unable to account for all the sums that had passed through his hands. Bonar Law, the new prime minister, began to investigate, and was told that Lord Astor had given Farquhar £200,000 to use at his discretion, of which Farquhar had given £40,000 to a charity in which the king was interested, splitting the remainder between the Conservative Party and Lloyd George. If Farquhar's rise through the peerage appears on the speedy side, Astor's, also under Lloyd George's patronage, was meteoric, his viscountcy in 1917 following his barony within fifteen months. Bonar Law failed to trace the missing £40,000 and fired Farquhar.

By this time the earl was 79 and, according to Lord Lincolnshire, "semi-idiotic". Bonar Law himself thought Farquhar was "gaga". But in May 1923 the king and queen dined with him at Grosvenor Square, and in August they called again. Two weeks later, he died. His will ran for pages, and included bequests to the king and queen, Queen Alexandra, the king's three sisters, his aunt, Princess Arthur of Connaught, the daughters of Princess Louise and no fewer than forty-eight members of the aristocracy. The estate was initially sworn for probate at £400,000. The king had been left anything he wished to choose from the contents of Castle Rising, the queen the entire contents of White Lodge.

Alas for Queen Mary's love of antiques, nobody got a sausage. Lord Farquhar's will proved not to be worth the paper it was written on. Every stick of furniture was mortgaged by debts, and the final value of his estate was nil. Even worse, he had acted as a trustee to the Fife estates (the duke had died in 1912), and £80,000 from that quarter was now discovered to be missing. His innocent co-trustee, the duke's widow, became liable for the debts, and she was, so Lord Lincolnshire reported, "open-mouthed in consequence". Having regained her royal composure, Princess Louise began sending off family portraits to Christie's. Another picture, belonging to the Howard family, came to add a disquieting postscript to the Farquhar saga. On repossessing Castle Rising from the king, whose sub-tenant Farquhar had been, the owners noticed that a painting by Crome had been repositioned high on the wall. When it was brought down to be cleaned it was found to be a copy.

If George V's friendship with Lord Farquhar was sullied by money, it was Lloyd George's political career that was finally ruined by finance, and if a single financial transaction proved more ruinous than any other it was one involving a multimillionaire, Sir Joseph Robinson, a most unpleasant, parsimonious man who had made his fortune out of South African gold. His purchase of a baronetcy from Campbell-Bannerman's government in 1908 had therefore been a bagatelle. So too had been his purchase of a house in Park Lane, together with Rembrandts and Romneys with which to furnish it. In 1911 Sir Joseph Robinson, Bt called on Mr J. Maundy-Gregory, who was at that time busy profiling "Men of the Day" in a magazine called *Mayfair*. Gregory thought to capitalize on his meeting with Robinson once he had established himself as an honours broker, and in turn called upon Sir Joseph in Park Lane. Robinson was by this time 82, but there seemed no reason to Gregory why he should not be interested in a seat in the House of Lords, even if he could not hear what was going on, for he also happened to be deaf. But Robinson was still as stingy as he had always been and, notwithstanding his age and his infirmity, he beat Gregory down from £50,000 to £30,000.

And so in the notorious 1922 Birthday Honours List a

barony for Robinson was announced — "for national and imperial services". He was also described as chairman of the Robinson South African Banking Company. On this occasion, the king and his private secretary would have needed to be exceptionally well briefed to have spotted, on perusing the list before publication, that the Robinson South African Banking Company had been liquidated seventeen years before. But the Palace might just have been expected, for their own sake, to have recollected — a detail that had seemingly slipped Lloyd George's memory — that in connection with another of his enterprises, the Randfontein Estates Company, Robinson had been convicted of fraud, fined £500,000 by the South African Supreme Court, and had his appeal turned down by the Judicial Committee of the Privy Council as recently as November 1921.

Lord Selborne announced that the country was faced with "a public scandal of the first magnitude". It was certainly faced with a public spectacle of private anguish. When accused during a House of Commons debate of having traded with the enemy, another of Lloyd George's potential peers, Sir Archibald Williamson, leapt to his feet in the Gallery and shouted, "That is a lie!" Realizing he had gone too far, the prime minister took the unprecedented step of sending an emissary to Robinson (who for some reason had forsaken his Park Lane mansion for a suite at the Savoy) to try to persuade him to decline the offer of a peerage — already of course announced in the press. Hard of hearing, he thought he was being pressed for more money, and got out his cheque book. After learning that the House of Lords were threatening to petition the king to refuse to grant letters patent, Robinson signed a letter already dictated for him, and that afternoon, 29 June, the letter declining the barony was read in the House of Lords by the Lord Chancellor, Lord Birkenhead, a man who had himself received expensive gifts from Maundy Gregory. "Little less than an insult to the Crown," was how George V described the amazing mess into which his prime minister had dragged the honours system when he wrote a letter personally to Lloyd George to tell him what he thought of the matter.

The Honours System

"Dear Prime Minister," the king wrote on 3 July: "I cannot conceal from you my profound concern at the very disagreeable situation which has arisen on the question of Honours.

"The Peerages which I was advised to confer upon Sir Joseph Robinson and Sir Archibald Williamson have brought things rather to a climax: though for some time there have been evident signs of growing public dissatisfaction on account of the excessive number of honours conferred; the personality of some of the recipients; and the questionable circumstances under which the honours in certain instances have been granted.

"You will remember that both in conversation and in written communications I have deprecated the ever increasing number of those submitted for the half-yearly Honours Gazette: and in recent years there have been instances in which honours have been bestowed where subsequent information has betrayed a lack of care in the enquiries made as to the fitness of the person selected for recognition.

"The case of Sir Joseph Robinson and all that it has evoked in the Debates in the House of Lords and in the newspaper reports of interviews given by him to Press representatives, must be regarded as little less than an insult to the Crown and to the House of Lords and may, I fear, work injury to the Prerogative in the public mind at home and even more in South Africa.

"I fully realize that the inordinate demands upon your time make it impossible for you, in spite of your marvellous capacity for work, personally to investigate the claims and qualifications of those persons whose names you submit for my approval for honours and rewards.

"But I do appeal most strongly for the establishment of some efficient and trustworthy procedure in order to protect the Crown and the Government from the possibility of similar painful if not humiliating incidents, the recurrence of which must inevitably consitute an evil, dangerous to the social and political well being of the State."

Maundy Gregory

How close was the king edging towards the truth when he referred in his letter to "the questionable circumstances under which the honours in certain instances have been granted"? Did he suspect they were being granted purely in exchange for cash? When he seemed to exonerate the prime minister from responsibility for investigating personally the claims and qualifications of those whose names he submitted, was this genuine kind-heartedness towards a prime minister who had at least extricated the country from the military shambles of the Great War, or can one detect here a touch of sarcasm? Lloyd George, after all, had no reason to investigate those whose names had particularly upset the king, short of making sure their cheques did not bounce. Given all the circumstances, it was a remarkably retrained missive.

As soon as Robinson's peerage seemed to be causing a fuss, Maundy Gregory went to ground, and although Lloyd-George's political career effectively came to an end four years later, Gregory's name was never mentioned. This was partly because he knew so much that a great many people went in fear and trembling of a wholesale leak of information. The only person who kept perfectly calm was Gregory himself. Having been cheated of his peerage, Robinson, not unnaturally, demanded the return of his £30,000. The chief whip, Charles McCurdy, asked Gregory if he knew what had become of it. "Of course I know what has become of it," Gregory replied. "I have spent it."

Maundy Gregory's heyday as an honours broker was certainly during the prime ministership of Lloyd George, but his activities continued under any available government, for the Liberal Party had never been alone in turning a blind eye to the origins of some of their funds and the motives of their benefactors. During the Lloyd George coalition, Conservative Party funds rose from £600,000 to £1,250,000, largely through the sale of honours. It was not until three years after Lloyd George's fall from power — which was occasioned in great measure by his overwhelming greed in the sale of honours — that the Honours (Prevention of Abuses) Act was passed, and it took the *Banker* a further two years to get round to describing many of Lloyd George's creatures as "gross illiterate profiteers, doubtful in their reputations, vulgar in their lives, who, to the shame of honour and decency, were shovelled into the House of Lords, created baronets and knights, merely upon the strength of the money they had obtained in preying upon England in the most awful crisis of her affairs".

The Prevention of Abuses Act was a direct outcome of a Royal Commission set up by Lloyd George in 1922 in response to the king's acute anxiety about the way the honours system had drifted into chaos. It sat under the chairmanship of Lord Dunedin and was charged with enquiring into the principles involved and the procedures followed in submitting names for honours. One of its recommendations was the setting up of an honours scrutiny committee to look into political honours, consisting of three privy councillors, but it made quite plain that the prime minister himself was responsible for the names he submitted to the king. One interesting piece of evidence gathered by the commission came from Lord Stamfordham, who told them the king would not even countenance approaches by members of the royal family on behalf of those they thought worthy of an honour. The king himself never initiated honours, other than the Royal Victorian Order and the Order of Merit, Stamfordham told the commission, for he believed that constitutionally all honours should be recommended by the prime minister. Eight years later, George V did, however, venture to suggest to Ramsay MacDonald that a certain famous inventor should receive a knighthood, and was cruelly snubbed for his pains. Downing Street was "snowed under" with applications, MacDonald's private secretary told Lord Stamfordham, a mean and ludicrous remark which drew from the king a plaintiff retort. "I only hope," he noted in his diary, "that the spade used will be a large one and the snow not too deep. As I so seldom ask for a knighthood, I really think that I might be treated with anyhow some consideration occasionally." In theory, the king could have conferred the accolade on anyone he chose, any time he chose and anywhere he chose. But he was scrupulous in his adherence to constitutional practice as it had evolved with the development of constitutional monarchy, and simply swallowed his pride, as he had so often been forced to do in the past.

Under the 1925 Prevention of Abuses Act it became an offence to accept "any gift, money or valuable consideration as an inducement or reward for procuring . . . the grant of a dignity or title of honour", and anyone who paid money for an honour was also liable for prosecution. So Maundy Gregory was compelled to diversify his operations, keeping his nose clean and his bank balance buoyant by effecting introductions to society hostesses, taking up fund-raising (among other charities, for King George's Fund for Sailors, of which the Duke of York was president) and selling foreign orders. It was not until 1933 that the Attorney-General got around to prosecuting him, and only then because Gregory had taken a foolhardy decision to try and obtain £10,000 for a knighthood from a retired naval officer, Edward Billyard-Leake. The man who was sent to 10 Hyde Park Terrace, the house Gregory shared with Edith Rosse, to arrest him was Detective Chief Inspector Arthur Askew; four years later he was to be in charge of security at the coronation of George VI.

Gregory's defiance of the new law was ill-considered because far from being a member of the *nouveaux riches*, Billyard-Leake was a close friend of the king's nephew, Lord Louis Mountbatten, and unlike so many of Gregory's clients who had stayed at home during the war to make their fortunes, Billyard-Leake had won the DSO, the Légion d'Honneur and the Croix de Guerre. Maundy Gregory in fact came to the conclusion that he had been persuaded to approach such an unlikely customer in a frame-up. The original plan was for the broker to plead guilty and receive a short, deterrent sentence. Far too many people, from the Earl of Scarborough down (he had been gullible enough to invite Gregory to become deputy director of a centenary appeal for the Order of the Hospital of St John of Jerusalem), were anxious for as little to come out in court as possible. But Gregory became so convinced that he had been duped that he determined to plead not guilty and fight the case. Norman Birkett, a future Lord Justice of Appeal and Nuremberg prosecutor, undertook to defend him, and wisely obtained a fee of £300 in advance. Lined up against Birkett in the magistrate's court were both the Attorney-General and the Director of Public Prosecutions, and in a desperate but unsuccessful attempt to induce Gregory to plead guilty, the Attorney-General agreed to a summary trial, involving on conviction only a maximum prison sentence of three months. After much bargaining behind the scenes, Gregory got two months and a fine of £50.

If the attempted sale of a peerage to Sir Joseph Robinson through the good offices of Maundy Gregory backfired on Lloyd George, Gregory's offer to procure a peerage for another baronet, Sir George Watson, also, like Robinson, a millionaire, was to have disastrous consequences for Gregory himself. In 1923, Watson had made over to Gregory bonds worth £30,000, redeemable in 1930. But still by 1930 Gregory had failed to conjure up the peerage, in 1926 even blaming the General Strike, saying it had "butted in and caused the entire side-tracking of our collection of names". But Gregory's luck ran out in 1930, the year for redemption. Not that that would have mattered very much in the normal way, for the good-natured and long-suffering Sir George had coughed up a further £4,000; unfortunately, however, 1930 was also the year in which Sir George elected to expire. His executors immediately called upon Gregory for their £30,000. He was faced with the choice of bluffing it out in court, with the defence that the £30,000 had been a gift, a story few would have chosen to believe, or of settling out of court — and facing financial ruin. He managed to buy time in January 1932 by repaying £10,000 and agreeing to produce a further £20,000 in two six-monthly instalments. The Prevention of Abuses Act now being in force, it was an almost impossible task.

Over the years, Gregory had helped Edith Rosse with her investments. On 19 August 1932, while London was cooking in a temperature of 83 degrees and Maundy Gregory was lunching at the Carlton Hotel with the King of Greece, Mrs Rosse, admittedly an alcoholic, and having attempted to cool off by drinking half a bottle of champagne, came over queer. In fact, so ill did she feel that she became convinced she was dying. Gregory was summoned by telephone from the Carlton. According to his own version of what transpired, shortly after his arrival at Hyde Park Terrace Mrs Rosse asked him to get pen and paper, and then dictated her will, which Gregory took down on the back of a menu he had mysteriously placed in his pocket before leaving the hotel. He was unable to find a pen, not, apparently, even in his own breast pocket, and so he wrote in pencil: "Everything I have, if anything happens to me to be left to Mr J. Maundy-Gregory to be disposed of as he thinks best and in accordance with what I should desire." This was witnessed by the housekeeper, Mrs L. Eyres, and Dr E.C. Plummer. Mrs Rosse signed it twice. It was a will, one may think, drafted in oddly pseudo-legal language for a dying lay woman to dictate.

At all events, it came into effect just twenty-six days later. Following the death of Edith Rosse on 14 September, Gregory failed to notify her relatives, and when a niece telephoned by chance on the day of Mrs Rosse's funeral, he even refused to reveal the cause of her death. Meanwhile, he had been touring potential burial grounds, alighting eventually on a graveyard adjacent to the Thames, well known for the frequency with which it was flooded. It was here, at Bisham, near Marlow, about as close to the water's edge as he could manage and in a grave dug "as shallow as possible", that he had Edith Rosse buried — in an unsealed coffin.

Did Maundy Gregory murder Edith Rosse? The circumstantial evidence seems almost overwhelming. After the niece, Ethel Davies, had approached Scotland Yard with her suspicions, Mrs Rosse's body was exhumed, six months after her burial and with ample time having passed for any traces of poison, assuming there had been any, to have been washed out by the Thames. Her post-mortem took three months, and after an inquest conducted with almost unbelievable inefficiency the coroner recorded an open verdict. By this time, her sole beneficiary was already working in the library at Wormwood Scrubs. He had run through his legacy of £18,865 18s 11d in eight weeks (it had, of course, gone to pay off debts), and it was surely because he still required a further £10,000 to silence Sir George Watson's executors in January 1933 that he had played his last and fatal card by approaching the impeccable Edward Billyard-Leake.[1]

After serving his prison sentence, J. Maundy-Gregory bestowed a knighthood on himself, became "Sir Arthur Gregory", and went to live in France. He made no serious attempt to evade the German invasion, was eventually interned, and died in hospital at St Denis on 28 September 1941. He was buried at the Ivry-Paris New Cemetery. His own will has disappeared.

---

1. The grant of administration was made to John Maundy-Gregory, "newspaper proprietor". A further grant of probate was made on 20 August 1934 to Frederick Saleman, a chartered accountant, for £187 16s 3d.

CHAPTER SEVEN

Who Gets What . . .

Looking through the photographs in the New Year Honours List, I am struck (as usual) by the quite exceptional ugliness and vulgarity of the faces displayed there. It seems to be almost the rule that the kind of person who earns the right to call himself Lord Percy de Falcontowers should look at best like an overfed publican and at worst like a tax collector with a duodenal ulcer.

George Orwell, writing in Tribune, 7 January 1944.

With Lloyd George safely returned to the backbenches, the advent of a Labour government in 1924, far from sending reactionary shivers down the spine of George V, seems to have inspired the benign and caring side of his nature. Writing to his mother on 17 February about the new ministers, he told her, "They have different ideas to ours as they are all socialists, but they ought to be given a chance & ought to be treated fairly." The king in fact treated his first Labour prime minister, Ramsay MacDonald, to a helpful little homily on how to behave, delivered by way of a memorandum, and in the course of drafting it the king grasped the opportunity of taking a new broom to the honours system. "It is hoped that a firm hand will be kept on the distribution of honours," MacDonald was told. "With the exception of the last Government [Stanley Baldwin's], the bestowal has been extravagant. Especial care should be taken with regard to appointments to the Privy

Council. Mr Gladstone said that a Privy Councillorship used to be regarded as a greater honour than a Peerage."

The king reminded MacDonald of one of the constitutional facts of life Lloyd George had so frequently overlooked, that before anyone was offered an honour the king's approval should be obtained, "until which time the individual in question should not be approached on the subject". George V also explained that he deprecated the bestowal of honours on ministers while in office. He added another interesting recommendation on his own initiative; excluding the Dominions, he told Ramsay MacDonald, no more than 16 baronetcies and 48 knighthoods should be conferred in a year.

George V was dealing with a socialist of moderate views. Far from taking the opportunity to send hordes of left-wing firebrands to the House of Lords to balance the Tory and Liberal benches, Ramsay MacDonald gratefully accepted the services of a Tory and two Liberal peers in his administration, and restricted his own first creations to two bachelors, Sydney Arnold and Brigadier C.B. Thomson (killed six years later in the R101 Airship disaster over France), and to Sir Sydney Olivier (uncle of the actor Laurence Olivier), who had no sons. All three had also been to public schools. When he came to form his second administration, in 1929, he only found it necessary to ennoble the new Lord Chancellor, Sir John Sankey, so that he could sit on the Woolsack, and to send the mild-mannered Fabian, Sidney Webb, to the House of Lords, as Lord Passfield. Although many of MacDonald's first cabinet colleagues were as rough-and-ready, in speech and manners, as any toiler in the class struggle could have wished, trade union leaders still had to wait some time to get themselves decked out in ermine.

Such are the absurdities of human nature, however, that even two men of good will and as clear in their own minds about the distribution of honours as George V and Ramsay MacDonald could not, it seems, avoid falling into a tangle. Thinking to please both the king and Sir Clive Wigram, who had succeeded Lord Stamfordham as private secretary, MacDonald proposed a peerage for Wigram in the King's

Who Gets What ...

Birthday Honours List of 1935, the year of the silver jubilee. The king however had taken against Sir Frederick Ponsonby, his keeper of the privy purse for twenty-one years, and a courtier whose services stretched back to the days when he was assistant private secretary to Queen Victoria. Although Ponsonby had received the KCVO in 1910, been advanced to GCVO in 1921 and had received the GCB in 1926, the king had no desire to give him a peerage, but he also realized he could hardly permit Wigram to receive a peerage if Ponsonby did not. This was explained by MacDonald to Wigram, who replied, "Your generous recommendation is evidently embarrassing to His Majesty and of course I could never dream of placing His Majesty in a difficult position after all he has done for me. At the same time I am sure you will agree that it is bad luck to be disposessed of a heritage through the vagaries of a colleague." MacDonald went back to the king, who very properly changed his mind, and in the nick of time Sir Frederick Ponsonby became Lord Sysonby. He died four months later.

Shortly before he, too, left the stage, George V told Ramsay MacDonald how well he had understood his refusal of a peerage on his retirement as prime minister in 1935, adding, perhaps a little unrealistically, that if he were *nouveau riche* the last thing he would do would be to run after a peerage. MacDonald was far from *nouveau riche*; he was hardly able to make ends meet, and he was also a man of principle. Not wishing to sport the prefix of a knighthood, he even declined the Thistle, an equivalent honour, for a Scotsman, of the Garter. Had MacDonald accepted he would have been the first commoner to enter the order.[1]

During the reign of George V, racial prejudice entered into the question of honours for Indians. A member of the royal household decided they were not, if knighted, entitled to the prefix "Sir", apparently on the ground that such knighthoods were honorary. As Indians were members of the Empire and

---

1. Prime ministers who have declined the Garter include Pitt the Younger, Sir Robert Peel and Neville Chamberlain, and initially Asquith, Churchill and Eden.

subjects of the king their knighthoods could in no way be regarded as honorary, and the king very sensibly reversed the decision. He shared with Queen Victoria an enlightened colour blindness when it came to questions of race or racial prejudice, a liberal tendency out of tune with certain members of his family and household. The Lord Chamberlain, in 1919, spotted Lady Diana Cooper sitting beside the Aga Khan at the Ritz, and delivered himself of the opinion that "the sight of natives entertaining smart society women was not a pleasant one". Queen Mary's brother, Prince Francis of Teck, refused to dine with Grand Duke Michael of Russia when he learned that the duke's wife was to be taken into dinner by an Indian prince. When Lord Lee of Fareham gave a garden party his wife recorded in her diary, "One thing Arthur was firm about was that he would not have any *Indians* asked." Yet Lee had the audacity to preside over a Royal Commission on the Indian Civil Service, and then to pester the government until he was made a Knight Grand Cross of the Star of India.

Bestowal of British honours on subjects of countries within the Commonwealth is today dependent upon the wishes of the individual countries. Generally speaking, honours are only accepted by monarchal nations, not by republics, and although monarchal, Canada declines any honour involving a title. Outside the Commonwealth it is possible for a citizen of a republic or a monarchy to receive an honorary British knighthood, but never a peerage. Examples include the American violinist Mr Yehudi Menuhin, KBE and the Dutch conductor, Mr Bernard Haitink, KBE. In 1976 the former foreign editor of *Le Figaro,* M. Roger Massip, was made CBE. In the same year, fourteen Americans were showered with honours, including KBEs for a former American ambassador to the United Kingdom, Mr Walter Annenberg, and for Mr Dean Rusk, and a CBE for Bob Hope, one of the Royal Family's favourite comedians. Even in the matter of honorary knighthoods, however, George V got himself bamboozled — by an American First World War correspondent for the *Daily Express,* Percival Phillips, who managed to slip through the net, receiving both the KBE and the accolade at Buckingham

Who Gets What...

Palace, and henceforth calling himself Sir Percival. After the second world war, the British government was often less than generous in honouring allied heroes. M. Yves Allain, one of the bravest members of the French Resistance, was thought worthy by his own country to receive, among other decorations, the Croix de Guerre with palm and the Légion d'Honneur, but although he had engineered an escape route for some 250 Allied airmen, Britain merely gave him an MBE.

The majority of British honours awarded to foreigners today form part and parcel of state visits, either at home or overseas. Should any British subject be offered a foreign or Commonwealth honour, permission to accept it is first required from the Queen, who will either refuse permission (the acceptance of honours from Iran, for example, has been suspended "until further notice"), grant what is known as unrestricted permission, or give permission to wear the insignia restricted to occasions particularly associated with the country concerned. Permission to wear a foreign order is granted inclusive of any British orders, not in addition to. A portrait was once painted of Edward VII wearing five Stars, the collar and Badge of the Garter, the Broad Ribbon and Badge of the KCVO and the Royal Victorian Chain, with the Sovereign's Badge of the Order of the Bath also round his neck. Today the maximum regalia permitted, no matter how many honours may have been received, is one Broad Ribbon and Badge, four Stars and three neck badges. Thus a garlanded proconsul like Lord Mountbatten, awarded four knight grand crosses in addition to the Garter (GCB, GCSI, GCIE and GCVO), always had to leave one of his five Stars at home.

A romantic and improbable range of foreign orders are available. From Albania one might receive the Order of the Partisan Star, from Bulgaria the Order of 9 September 1944. China has on offer the Air Force Order of the Ancient Symbols, while friends of Japan may sport the Supreme Order of the Chrysanthemum. Liberia keeps its options open with the Order of Knighthood of Pioneers of the Republic. It seems unlikely that the present fad for small families will result in any subject of Her Britannic Majesty receiving the Russian Order of the Glory of Motherhood, although a lady responsible for the fostering of 350 children, Mrs June Gaunt, was made MBE in 1979. More glamorous perhaps would be a letter from King Bhumibol Adulyadej of Thailand offering the Order of the White Elephant.

A white elephant, as some believe, rather closer to home, the House of Lords, seems to become the focus every few years for attempts at reconstituting the nature and functions of Parliament, in which, however, few people's hearts are truly engaged. Generally speaking, objections to the Lords have been based on two principal factors: their right to override the elected Commons, that is to say, their legislative powers; and the composition of the House, in other words, its non-elective and hereditary element. So far as the legislative powers of the House of Lords are concerned, the 1911 Parliament Act left the Lords with little to do but exercise limited delaying tactics, but they were still left with the power to reject an Order in Council or a statutory instrument which needed the assent of both Houses to become law, together with what were known as negative prayers, orders which automatically became effective on promulgation but which could be nullified by a decision of either House. In effect, if a government's legislative programme is particularly heavy or complicated — and these days almost all governments' programmes are — detailed consideration of a Bill in the House of Lords, resulting in amendments and even government defeats, can have a serious, and often salutary, effect on the eventual outcome of Parliamentary Bills.

So far as composition of the House is concerned, in 1917 a committee under Lord Bryce recommended that 246 members of the Upper House should be elected by the House of Commons and that a quarter of the Upper House should be chosen from existing hereditary peers by a joint committee of the two Houses. Needless to say, nothing came of this complex compromise. By and large, what has happened is that some pertinent issue has arisen and talks have been held, or else the House of Commons has satisfied itself with a sarcastic exchange of views and abuse, Labour supporters who swear that they find the hereditary principle indefensible have accepted life peerages, and the battle-cries have died away again.

But in 1967 all-party talks under the chairmanship of the Lord Chancellor did seem to be making progress, along the lines of streamlining membership of the House of Lords (the Anglican bishops, for example, were to be reduced in number, with the full approval of the Archbishop of Canterbury, Dr Michael Ramsey) and phasing out the hereditary element by abolishing membership for all new accessions. But they were abruptly called off by the prime minister, Harold Wilson, furious because in a successful attempt to defeat an Order in Council imposing a total trade ban on Rhodesia, the Conservative peers had whipped up members of the House of Lords some of whom had neither spoken nor voted since taking their seat. This was a clear case of mockery being made of democracy, of men born in a certain bedroom claiming the right to frustrate the intentions of an elected Commons, and a number of Conservative peers were so disturbed by the tactic that they even supported the Labour government, who now took the view that legislation to curtail the powers of the Lords was more urgent than to deal with the hereditary principle. "Comprehensive and radical legislation" was threatened by Mr Wilson. However, the Lord Chancellor, Lord Gardiner, and the Leader of the Lords, Lord Shackleton, persuaded the Cabinet that it would not be meaningful to change the powers of the House of Lords while leaving its composition based in the main on hereditary membership, so in February 1969 a Bill received its second reading which proposed a two-tier structure for the House of Lords, one list of peers with a vote and one without. Peers who could vote would be confined to first creations (a move intended to restrict voting peers eventually to life peers, although no legislation was envisaged actually prohibiting the future creation of hereditary peerages, suspended *sine die* in 1965), and even these voting peers would be required to prove a reasonable attendance record and would be subject to a retirement age — an ironic suggestion in the light of Lord Shinwell's attendance at the House in 1984 looking spruce and sprightly on his hundredth birthday, not to mention the astonishing *tour de force* a few weeks later when Lord Stockton, in making his maiden speech at the age of 90 without a single note, held the House spellbound for thirty-two minutes and received an unprecedented standing ovation. Non-voting peers were to consist of those who held their seats through hereditary succession, and it was envisaged that the hereditary element would eventually be abolished by refusing membership to new successions.

So far as the powers of the House of Lords were concerned, they would be allowed to delay a House of Commons Bill for six months, and their power to reject a statutory order was to be overruled. During the second reading, a coalition of the Labour left and the Tory right, led by Mr Michael Foot and Mr Enoch Powell, combined to oppose the Bill. It was passed on second reading, gaining support from the Tory front bench, but so many amendments were tabled by its opponents in committee stage that nine days of parliamentary time and eighty-eight hours of committee debate were consumed, with the result that the government's major legislative programme got into so much difficulty that the Bill was dropped. Once again the entire question of abolishing hereditary membership of Parliament had been shelved.

Going in the other direction, Mrs Margaret Thatcher made it clear that she reserved the right to nominate hereditary peers given the opportunity and the inclination, and in the Dissolution Honours List of 1983 she revived a traditional viscountcy for the Speaker of the House of Commons, following this up with an earldom for a former prime minister, Mr Harold Macmillan. It has to be assumed that Mr Macmillan had previously declined a hereditary peerage on resigning his seat in the Commons, but many men of 90 acquiesce in actions they have resisted at a younger age. Mrs Thatcher's first hereditary peerages for eighteen years were not only sparse but cautious; the Speaker was a bachelor, and another recipient of a viscountcy, Mr William Whitelaw, although married had no heir.

Over the decade 1975-84 the numbers of new life peers

Who Gets What . . .

created each year has run at a fairly consistent level: about ten. In no honours list other than the Birthday Honours of 1979, which was Mrs Thatcher's second list and contained eleven life peers and three life peeresses, has the number exceeded six. In January 1981 it was down to two, and in the summer of 1984 there were no life peers at all. In addition to the prime minister's list, the two annual lists contain appointments by the Queen to the Royal Victorian Order and lists relating specifically to the Diplomatic Service, the armed forces and such far-flung outposts of colonial splendour as Australia, New Zealand, Papua New Guinea, Mauritius, Fiji and Grenada.

So far as the prime ministers' lists have been concerned, appointments to all grades of award over the past ten years have varied very little. The Companionship of Honour is simply filled as and when a vacancy occurs. Admittance to the Privy Council for people other than those who would expect to be sworn by virtue of their office has been kept down to about six a year. Knights Bachelor have averaged out at around sixty per annum, only some dozen more than George V told Ramsay MacDonald he thought appropriate sixty years ago, but their numbers (thirty-eight in the combined Jubilee and Birthday Honours List of 1977, and never falling below twenty-one, in January 1979) compare most unfavourably with the meagre average of about three admissions each year of women as Dames Commander of the Order of the British Empire.

KBEs (again, as monitored in the prime minister's list) have run at a modest 0.5 per cent on average per annum, and in the past ten years there have been just three promotions to GBE. KCBs handed out from Downing Street in the past decade have run to just under seven a year, with promotions to GCB occurring on average only once a year. Appointments to the Order of the Bath as a commander have been very steady at around thirty-six a year, but while commanders of the Order of St Michael & St George average out over the past ten years at five a year, these seem in fact to be dropping from ten a year under Mr James Callaghan to two a year under Mrs Thatcher. Those admitted as commanders, officers and members of the

The Honours System

Order of the British Empire fluctuate sufficiently each year to indicate that there is no firmly fixed quota it is felt necessary to fill, but they run on average at about 320, 400 and 720 respectively. In the summer of 1984, for instance, those who were numbered so prominently among the MBEs were a Dorset fire officer, someone who had given service to the Jewish community in Leeds, the chairman of the Lambeth Sea Cadet Corps, a senior executive officer at Customs and Excise, someone who works at the London Air Traffic control centre, a pharmacist at a health centre in Lancashire, a police chief superintendent on Merseyside, the head government butler and a woman who writes children's books.

Altogether, under the prime minister's patronage alone some 1,480 citizens, a number of them already decorated with Stars and Badges, receive an honour of some sort every year. By the time the Garter, the Thistle, the Order of Merit and the Royal Victorian Order have been topped up from time to time, and recommendations from Commonwealth prime ministers, heads of departments in the Foreign Office and the Queen's cousins (members of all the Royal Households stand in line for membership of the Royal Victorian Order after certain years of service) have been taken into account, the total annual figure is approaching 3,000. Where peerages and knighthoods are concerned, wives and children come in for titles, and allowing for spouses, children, parents and grandchildren, never mind friends, the number of gratified subjects directly involved in the award of an honour each year cannot be less than 25,000.

Who are the lucky recipients? Civil servants, diplomats and members of the armed forces, so long as they perform the jobs they are paid to do to the satisfaction of their paymaster, the state, receive honours as a matter of course, in the time-honoured tradition of Buggin's turn. Britain's influence in the world of international nuclear politics may now be minimal, but the colonial atmosphere still enshrined in the Foreign Office, at home and overseas, appeals enormously to countries with a less well defined and marshalled pageantry, and it is felt that if a Foreign Office official is to go to an embassy reception he cannot do so shorn of a ribbon round his neck or across his shoulder. It would disappoint his host. Accordingly, in June 1984 Her Majesty's Ambassador in Baghdad received the KBE, Her Majesty's Ambassador in Athens the KCMG. Her Majesty's Ambassador in Kathmandu, clearly a junior appointment, got the CMG to be going on with. The vice-consul at the British Embassy in Tunisia received the MBE, for she still has a lot of leg-work ahead of her. At the top end of the scale, Sir Michael Butler, the United Kingdom's Permanent Representative to the EEC, was advanced to Knight Grand Cross of the Order of St Michael & St George.

If a general is to appear to proper effect when taking the salute, especially now that the opportunities for generals to earn medals are few and far between, he too is deemed inappropriately dressed unless he has a Star on his chest. Hence in June 1984 the Deputy Colonel of the Royal Anglican Regiment, who happens to be a lieutenant-general, got the KCB. Four CBs out of six awarded in the army list went to major-generals. Three brigadiers, three colonels and an army chaplain got the CBE.

When those who normally expect to receive honours wrapped up in their increments fail to toe the line they can expect to have their CBE or whatever is due withheld. In 1981 a number of civil servants (all of whom feature in the prime minister's list) engaged in a pay dispute, much to the displeasure of Mrs Thatcher, who made it known to permanent secretaries that the names of anyone who took part should not be sent to her for inclusion either in the Birthday Honours List of that year or the New Year Honours List of 1982. Mr Alan Williams, MP, the Labour spokesman on the civil service, accused her of "sheer bitchy vindictiveness". Those who took part in the industrial action were inevitably fairly young and therefore in relatively low grades, and it seems likely that those who missed out on honours would normally have appeared with MBEs and OBEs. In the 1980 Birthday Honours List, 141 civil servants appeared, in the 1981 New Year Honours List, 140, and as the number of civil servants featured in June 1981 was reduced to 120 it would appear reasonable to deduce that altogether between thirty to forty civil servants who took part in the pay dispute were denied their time-earned honour. With new recruits already on the ladder of promotion, their chances of regaining a place in the queue may have been jeopardized for ever.

The striking civil servants have not been the only expectant recipients of honours to have had their ambitions thwarted by Mrs Thatcher. In 1980 a number of British athletes attended the Olympics held in Moscow following the Russian invasion of Afghanistan, against the express wishes of the government, and then made a great fuss when not so much as an MBE fell into their laps in the 1981 New Year Honours List. "They opted for Olympic cake on a Soviet plate," the *Daily Telegraph* reminded them. "What self-respect can they have now to be bawling after British jam."

A former leader of the Labour Party, Mr Michael Foot, also had his knuckles rapped by Mrs Thatcher when in 1983, following his party's election defeat, he sent her a list of twenty-seven Labour supporters he wished to see ennobled in the Dissolution Honours List, in order, he said, to increase the Labour Party's diminished strength in the House of Lords. Mrs Thatcher took the view that such numbers were without precedent (which they were), out of all proportion to the occasion and might in fact adversely affect the Tory majority in the Upper House. Since 1959, no party had nominated more than nine new peers for a dissolution honours list, the purpose of which is to create peers for political purposes, not by way of reward for personal services, as is permissible with resignation honours. Mr Foot was on weak ground for another reason: committed to the eventual abolition of the House of Lords, he had consistently declined to nominate Labour peers when he had the opportunity, thus in large measure being responsible for the decline in his party's representation in the Lords. In the event, Mr Foot had to withdraw eighteen nominations and content himself with nine new peers, among them Sir Harold Wilson.

In June 1984 three Companions of Honour were chosen by

the prime minister: Lord Eccles, a former minister of education, Sir Arnold Powell, an architect, and Professor Friedrich von Hayek, an economist. Two equally worthy but rather dull men became privy councillors, the Hon. Adam Butler, rewarded no doubt for a stint as Minister of State in Northern Ireland, and Mr John Stanley, Minister of State for the Armed Forces, who also happened to be parliamentary private secretary to Mrs Thatcher from 1976-9. The prime minister's choice of knights bachelor included the principal of the London Business School, the chairman of the Countryside Commission, the chairman of the Farm Animal Welfare Council, the president of the Law Society (an annual appointment, every holder of which, for no good reason, gets a knighthood automatically), the secretary of the Agricultural and Food Research Council, the Governor of the Bank of Scotland, the chairman of the Oxford Regional Health Authority, the city editor of the *Daily Mail,* the chairman of the Merseyside Development Corporation, the chairman of the Post Office and the chairman of Glyndebourne. The fact that the Post Office has been known to take thirteen days to transport a first-class letter across London and that the prime minister is never known to have been to the opera just shows how many minds go to make up the honours list.

Also in Mrs Thatcher's list were three prominent industrialists. Such people have appeared before, and their names have in recent years caused consternation at the Labour Research Department, who decided to monitor the correlation between donations received by the Conservative Party from industrial firms in the years 1979-83 and peerages and knighthoods awarded to industrialists in the years 1980-83. They found that of forty-one directors of private companies awarded peerages or knighthoods during that period, twenty-eight came from companies which had contributed £2,756,366 to the Conservative Party in just four years. Out of eighteen companies that had given £90,000 or more to the Conservative Party between 1979-83, the directors of fourteen companies had been honoured by Mrs Thatcher. These firms had together contributed £1,859,756 to the Conservative

The Honours System

Party, a sum that represented an estimated 23 per cent of the party's income.

Several of those industrialists who received life peerages during the period under investigation are household names. In 1980, for instance, the year that Sir Robert McAlpine's various companies contributed £33,000 to the Tory Party, he went to the Lords. So did Mr Victor Matthews of Trafalgar House, whose business concerns in three years paid £120,000 into the Tory coffers. Sir Charles Forte of Trust House Forte fame and fortune was elevated in 1982, having that year put his signature on cheques in favour of the Conservative Party to the tune of £37,500, part of a total payment over three years of £96,000. Sir Marcus Sieff of Marks and Spencer, not all of whose satisfied customers presumably vote Conservative, spent £20,500 on the Conservative Party in 1980 and he too went to the Lords. Sir Arnold Weinstock of GEC wrote out a one-off cheque for £50,000 in 1980 and that year he received a peerage. But some of these sums may seem trivial compared to the amount paid to the Tory Party between 1979-82 by British and Commonwealth Shipbuilding — £218,581. The final payment, of £95,810, was made in 1982, the year Sir William Cayzer became a peer of the realm.

Under Mrs Thatcher's patronage, knighthoods too have been bestowed in profusion on those in charge of companies favourably disposed towards the Conservative Party. Allied-Lyons contributed £228,000 to the party in three years, and in 1981 Mr Keith Showering became Sir Keith. Sums ranging between £102,175 and £125,000 were paid during the same period by Wimpey, Glaxo, NEI and Racal, and all four had an executive knighted. In 1980 GEC made a donation of £50,000, seemingly their first and last; in the very same year, Mr Robert Clayton became Sir Robert. It has to be said that firms such as the Macfarlane Group, the Prudential, Rio Tinto Zinc, Sainsbury, Shell and Tesco that have received letters from Downing Street offering their directors knighthoods have paid no money into party funds at all. Yet the coincidental numbers of peerages and knighthoods received by the staff of certain firms that have made enormous

Who Gets What . . .

contributions indicate a system of purchasing honours with shareholders' profits.

The difference between Mrs Thatcher's methods of raising party funds and rewarding contributors and Lloyd George's seems only to have been one of refinement; in Mrs Thatcher's case, she dispensed with the middleman. In principle, the objectives were identical. Rumbled by the Labour Research Department, she immediately agreed to a request from the Political Honours Scrutiny Committee for a tightening up of vetting procedure. The matter was raised in the House of Commons under the ten-minute rule on 6 December 1983 by a Labour MP, Mr Austin Mitchell, but little fuss seems to have been made, and compared to the uproar engendered by Harold Wilson's resignation honours list, or any of the other honours scandals of the past, Mrs Thatcher's apparent sale of honours for party purposes, on the face of it a blatant prostitution of the honours system, caused scarcely a ripple on the surface of a society by now grown cynical in such matters to the point of inertia.

The 1984 Birthday Honours List contained among the prime minister's choice of knights bachelor three politicians rewarded "for political services", the Conservative members of Parliament for Harborough, Harrow West and Maidstone. They were sound, safe men who had nursed their constituencies for a quarter of a century. Mrs Thatcher owed them nothing personally; she may scarcely have known them. Their political careers had been without distinction; none had held ministerial office. They were being honoured by the prime minister in the Queen's name for good conduct and loyal service to their party, for serving as reliable lobby fodder, for not rocking the boat. Their constituency party and their wives were being thanked too. They were quite simply receiving political honours as a means of keeping the backbenches quiet and happy; if Sir John this year — and all three now are — why not Sir Henry or Sir William next?

Mrs Thatcher was merely re-enacting a custom followed far more lavishly in the past. Between 1959-64, Mr Harold Macmillan and Sir Alec Douglas-Home — a baronet himself

The Honours System

— conferred sixty-seven baronetcies and knighthoods upon Conservative backbenchers, but Mrs Thatcher would have noted that her immediate predecessor as leader of the Conservative Party, Mr Edward Heath, disliked the idea of political honours to the extent that between 1970-73 only nine knighthoods (excluding those traditionally bestowed on government lawyers) were handed out. Writing in *The Times* on 24 August 1973, the Tory MP for Aldershot, Mr Julian Critchley, asked, "If this goes on, how will Mr Pym [Francis Pym, then the chief whip] be able to keep us in the House after ten o'clock?" He was making out the age-old case for political honours, based on the argument that without the hope of an honour, the loyalty of party hacks cannot be relied on. "Mr Macmillan," he reminded his readers (and they almost certainly included the MP for Finchley), "who has read his Trollope, knows that patronage is the lubricant of public life. . . . In the past the party has sustained loyalty by the gift of a bauble. A Tory party without its Knight of the Shires would be like a ship without its ballast."

Mr Critchley went on to admit, "There might not have been much merit in a political knighthood but there was no harm in it. We do not operate a spoils system. We are paid a modest salary and expected to do our duty. The 'K', when it came," he continued, now thoroughly enthralled with his special pleading, as though members of parliament were half-starved social workers spurned by society despite their shining virtues, "was a boon to the Member's wife, and a blessing to the Member himself, at a time when his more curmudgeonly constituents were beginning to ask pointedly after his health."

At this point, Mr Critchley let off the hand-brake, slipped into fourth gear and careered towards the cliff. "If ambition," he wrote, "is the engine of the public good, then vanity is its starting-handle. Governorships have gone with empire. The number of peerages awarded to Tories has fallen over the same period [1970-73] from 43 to four — and all those are of the second class. We are turning the Lords into an old folks' home. Baronetcies have vanished altogether. Is then an MP, who must keep the hours of a street-walker; who is understood to be — if the public is to be believed — either impotent or corrupt; who spends the best years of his life listening to Minister's speeches, and to the complaints of his constituents; is he to receive as his only reward after 20 years of service a signed photograph of Jim Prior? Surely not."

He concluded with the truly tragic observation that Members were no longer beating a trail to Mr Pym's door in search of honours, for the well had gone dry.

Small wonder that, with a terrible warning like that ringing in her ears, Mrs Thatcher announced on 26 November 1979 that she was to reintroduce honours for political services. They had been abolished by Harold Wilson in 1966, reintroduced by Mr Heath (although not on a scale to satisfy most of his backbenchers) in 1970 and again abolished by Mr Wilson in 1974. Mrs Thatcher invited the leader of the Opposition, Mr James Callaghan, and the Liberal leader, Mr David Steel, to submit recommendations. Mr Callaghan declined. At the same time, Mrs Thatcher told the House of Commons she did not exclude the possibility of reintroducing hereditary peerages, a suggestion that led Mr Patrick Montague-Smith, the editor of *Debrett's*, to comment that it would be a good thing as it would allow young people who would not otherwise expect to go to the Lords to have the opportunity to make a contribution there. So far, there has been a distinct dearth of teenage barons; the nearest Mrs Thatcher has got to fulfilling Mr Montague-Smith's prophecy of a revival in medieval concepts of life expectancy was to give a knighthood in June 1983 to Mr Terry Burns, the 39-year-old chief executive adviser to the Treasury.

As good as her word, in her first New Year Honours List Mrs Thatcher bestowed honours on fifty of her fellow Conservatives. Six Liberals joined in the bonanza. Not all the new Tory knights were MPs. They included the prime minister's speech-writer, the editor of the *Sunday Express* (probably the most viciously reactionary journalist in Fleet Street) and somebody called Mr D.P. Sells of Royston. Lord Thorneycroft got the CH; Lord St Aldwyn, Conservative chief whip in the House of Lords for more than twenty years, was made a Knight Grand Cross of the Order of the British Empire. OBEs went to a pair of sanctimonious sons of the establishment, Mr Cliff Richard and Mr Tom Fleming. The list ran to 702 awards, people in local services receiving 235, servants of the state 141, teachers 36, exporters 22, the police 19 and nurses 13.

Over the next twelve months, Mr Hugo Young, political editor of the *Sunday Times,* kept an eye on the revival of political honours, and when the New Year Honours List for 1981 was published he swung into action. Already Mrs Thatcher had honoured eighteen backbenchers "for political services", compared with the nine Mr Heath had singled out during the whole of his premiership. Mr Young commented, "Once again, in fact, Mrs Thatcher takes her lesson from the failures of her predecessor as Tory leader. Honours are only the most delicious of the seductions she has to offer in her cultivation of her backbench members. She has sensibly given a high priority to this ever since she watched Ted Heath destroyed by his steady refusal to give the time of day to many MPs, let alone reward them."

Customarily, Mr Young pointed out, an unblemished reputation was pretty well the only requirement for a political knighthood. But he cited the case of a new knight whose reputation, he said, was not absolutely and one hundred per cent without blemish — Sir Peter Emery, the Member of Parliament for Honiton, whose excessive profits made out of a publicly financed driving school set up to improve the safety of North Sea oil and gas operations had been reported by the Public Accounts Committee of the House of Commons as recently as July 1980. "Almost nothing," Mr Young remarked, "seems to stand between a loyal, ageing Conservative backbencher and his gong."

The pattern of Mrs Thatcher's political awards, according to Mr Young, was that almost to a man they were "old, dry, obscure, Thatcherite and unremarkable". But, he said, Mr Emery broke that mould. He had tangled with the Public Accounts Committee and come off worst. "If Emery can get one, the aspiring Tory K must be saying, then there's hope for

Who Gets What . . .

me as well. Which is precisely the atmosphere any sensible prime minister, facing a major rebellion over the budget and other matters, would want to engender."

Twice a year the honours lists come in for editorial comment from the press (on 31 December 1984, the quite unexceptional New Year Honours List for 1985 made the lead news story on the front page of *The Times*), and any journalist hard up for an idea can be relied on to turn out a piece on the subject: why are Dames so called; why is not the entire *corps de ballet* at Covent Garden awarded the MBE; why not a new order for sportsmen; is it not time to abolish the House of Lords, the Queen, the prime minister's hairdresser, the entire honours system? But no honours list since 1922 has encouraged such reems of rage and derision as Mr Harold Wilson's resignation list of 1976.

To some extent the origins of the furore lay in Mr Wilson's earlier decision, in May 1974, to recommend a peerage for Mrs Marcia Williams, since 1956 his personal and political secretary. There had been a rumour in March of that year, vehemently denied from Downing Street, that Mr Wilson was planning a life peerage for Mrs Williams, the most influential member of what had become known as his kitchen cabinet, and by definition someone with the opportunity to make plenty of enemies as well as friends. But in April she had been at the centre of what David McKie described in the *Guardian* as a "fierce and bruising political controversy", set off by newspaper disclosures of property deals involving slag heaps in Lancashire said to have been carried out by her brother Mr Tony Field, also a former member of Mr Wilson's personal staff. Mrs Williams was named as a director of the company involved, and she had to be defended by Mr Wilson in the House of Commons. Whether Mr Wilson had intended offering his secretary a seat in the House of Lords all along, or whether he was tempted to do so in the aftermath of angry exchanges in the Commons, to show his contempt for the attacks on Mrs Williams and his continuing loyalty to her, will probably never be known. At all events, the announcement of her peerage (she became Lady Falkender) drew fire from all sides, some of it unquestionably motivated by anti-feminism. After all, she was a "secretary"; what place had such a creature in the House of Lords? "The most exciting news since Caligula made his horse a consul" was the most ingenious insult the Tory MP for Rutland and Stamford, Mr Kenneth Lewis, could think up. Equally predictable was Mr William Hamilton's contribution to the debate: "This just confirms my view that the sooner we get rid of the bloody nonsense of the honours list, the better. It is now the subject of hilarious cynicism."

But Mr Wilson had reserved his best surprises for his resignation honours list, due out shortly after he had stepped down from the leadership of the Labour Party on 16 March 1976. But before the list was officially announced on 27 May (rumours that a delay of more than two months had been caused because the Political Honours Scrutiny Committee had objected to three names on it were later denied by Mr Wilson) leaks appeared in the press, something which never occurs with the two annual lists, and for which no explanation has ever been given. And the leaks were not purely idle press speculation; they proved to be almost entirely accurate. The list contained forty-two names, among them nine life peers, the elevation of four of whom — Sir Lew Grade, Sir Bernard Delfont, Sir Joseph Kagan and Sir George Weidenfeld — were foretold in the *Sunday Times*. The same paper tipped Mr Sigmund Steinberg and Mr James Goldsmith (a former supporter of the Tory Party) for peerages, but in the event they only received knighthoods. A tongue in cheek award of the OBE went to the impersonator Mike Yarwood, knighthoods to two second-tier actors, John Mills and Stanley Baker, membership of the Privy Council to Mr Len Murray, general secretary of the TUC, and an MBE to Miss Peggy Field — the sister of Lady Falkender.

Two days before the list was officially published, Mr Bernard Levin felt sufficiently confident of the accuracy of some of the names leaked to pretend to leap to Mr Wilson's defence in a fine flurry of sarcasm. In an article in *The Times* he affected to trounce those who had seen fit to criticize the former prime minister and his nominees, and in glowing terms

Who Gets What . . .

produced a précis of their worthiness to enter the Upper House of Parliament. "Take Sir George Weidenfeld, for instance," Mr Levin wrote:

"The services he has done to British publishing with the success of his distinguished house [Weidenfeld and Nicolson] have already been rightly rewarded with a knighthood; it is being said that there can therefore be no good reason for now giving him a peerage. The kindest thing I can say about such comment is that it is simply ignorant — ignorant, that is, of Sir George's selfless and devoted work among the poor of Calcutta. Mother Teresa herself has paid eloquent tribute to the way in which Sir George, dressed in rags, night after night went about comforting the homeless, the hungry, the dying; to some he brought a blanket, to some food, to those beyond earthly help spiritual solace. Let the critics say what they have to show in their own lives that can be put beside the two years Sir George spent in this work, or what comparable understanding of the human condition they could bring to Parliament in the unlikely event of their finding themselves there.

"Or there is Sir Joseph Kagan; comment on his forthcoming elevation to the peerage has not only suggested that he is entirely unqualified for any participation in the legislature, and that in so far as his services to British industry (and to exports) deserved reward they have already been rewarded with his knighthood, but have taken on an unpleasantly snobbish flavour, several none-too-subtle suggestions having been made to the effect that he is 'nothing but a mackintosh-manufacturer'.

"In the first place, they also serve who do nothing but manufacture mackintoshes; would Sir Joseph's critics prefer the nation to get wet whenever it rains? But, far more important, the criticism is singularly ill-placed. If a test of fitness for a seat in Parliament is required, it would be hard to think of anyone who could pass it more easily than Sir Joseph, author of those monumental works of political, economic and constitutional history and philosophy, *The*

Law and the Constitution, The Open Society and its Enemies, The Wealth of Nations, Reflections on the Revolution of our Times, The Acquisitive Society, The Village Labourer, The Future of Socialism, The Labour Government: 1964-70, The Decline and Fall of the Roman Empire, The Road to Serfdom and *Sailing: a Course of my Life.* And that is to say nothing of Sir Joseph's achievements as a portrait-painter, mountaineer, High Court Judge and surgeon, nor his Presidency of the St John's Ambulance Brigade and Chairmanship of the Army Benevolent Fund.

"If Sir Joseph Kagan is almost embarrassingly well-supplied with qualifications for an honour, how much more so is another of those at present being reclamatively discussed, Mr James Goldsmith. When even so careful and reputable a commentator as Mr George Hutchinson can say, as he did on this page last Saturday, that he 'cannot think of a single reason', and that he can 'discover no grounds whatever' why Mr Goldsmith should have a title, it is clear that the rot has gone far. Not a single reason? No grounds whatever? What then of Mr Goldsmith's purchase for the nation of Rembrandt's *Aristotle Contemplating the Bust of Homer*? What of a man who has, as Mr Goldsmith has, endowed (entirely out of his own pocket) no fewer than 22 University Chairs, founded a chain of old people's homes in almost all the principal cities of Britain, and for three successive years covered the entire deficit of the Royal Opera House, thus enabling the Arts Council to put the available funds to other uses? And let it not be said that these are all actions which, admirable though they are, require only money, and that since Mr Goldsmith is an immensely wealthy man, even such generosity in the national interest should not entitle him to a peerage. What of Mr Goldsmith's activities, to which he devotes many hours a week, on behalf of the Church's Commission on Gambling? What of his exemplary courage in persuading the Balcombe Street gunmen to surrender to the authorities? What of the three gold medals he won for Britain at the last Olympic Games? What of his work as a Methodist lay preacher, a Marriage Guidance Counsellor, a Special Constable and a member of the International Council for Bird Preservation (British Section)? Above all, what of the example he sets, particularly to young people, by the modesty, dignity and lack of ostentation in his personal life — in such striking contrast to many other very wealthy men?

"The recent Festival Hall performance by Sir Lew Grade and Sir Bernard Delfont of Bach's Double Violin Concerto would alone entitle them both to the peerages they are apparently going to get; recognition of Mr Sigmund Sternberg's services to British philately is long overdue; and as for the knighthood for Mr Jarvis Astaire [a sports promoter], I can think of few more worthy recipients of an honour than this gifted dancer, singer and actor who has given so much pleasure to so many cinemagoers."[2]

Mr Levin's colleague George Hutchinson returned to the attack on 29 May, to assert that no honours list, resignation or otherwise, had ever been attended by such farce. Who, he asked, could wish for inclusion in a roll-call giving rise to such universal astonishment and derision? He declared that Sir Harold (the Queen had given him the Garter) had demeaned the office of prime minister and embarrassed his successor, James Callaghan. He had likewise embarrassed the Crown. As if that were not enough, poor Sir Harold was told he had also injured the Labour Party, and thereby the Government. In fact, Mr Hutchinson asserted, Sir Harold had brought so much discredit to the honours system that it might not survive in its present form. After explaining that it might be as well if Lady Falkender were to lie low for a while, for she could hardly be exonerated (Mr Hutchinson failed to say in what respect Lady Falkender could hardly be exonerated; her alleged crimes were not so much as mentioned), Mr Hutchinson drew blood — much of it blue — with better aimed shots at the strangely right-wing affiliations of some of

2. Mr Astaire's predicted knighthood did not materialize. Sir George Weidenfeld had published the memoirs of Lady Falkender. Lord Kagan went to prison for fraud.

those whom Sir Harold had asked the Queen to honour. They included Sir James Goldsmith, "a declared contributor to Tory funds", and James Hanson "who is immensely rich [and] has hitherto supported the Conservatives". He cited too as probable supporters of the Tory Party Sir Lew Grade and Wilson's doctor, Sir Joseph Stone, both ennobled; Stone's brother, Hutchinson pointed out, was none other than the Tory Party's treasurer, Lord Ashdown.

An assault from a right-of-centre journalist was perhaps to be expected; a far greater shock for Sir Harold Wilson must have been a motion signed by over hundred Labour MPs — a third of the Party's membership of the Commons — attacking his list. The motion rather feebly called on the chairman of the Parliamentary Labour Party to make it clear that the party had no responsibility for the resignation honours list, a fact anyone with the smallest working knowledge of parliamentary affairs would have understood perfectly well.

If Sir Harold had hoped that his own quiet retirement to the backbenches, warmly wrapped in his Garter mantle, and the bland and unsensational leadership of the party by Mr Callaghan, would enable the rumpus over his honours list to die the natural death of every political indiscretion, he was mistaken. The whole affair blew up again in February 1977 when his former press secretary, Mr Joe Haines, published a book called *The Politics of Power,* in which he alleged that the now notorious list had in fact been drawn up by Lady Falkender — "in her own hand on the lavender-coloured notepaper she often used". It was clearly time for settling old scores; while acknowledging that Lady Falkender could have made her way on merit into the Cabinet, Mr Haines described her as "the telphone tyrant" who "demoralized not only those who had to work with her, but Harold Wilson also". The previous year, Lady Falkender had written in a letter to *The Times* that the list had been "Sir Harold Wilson's list and his alone". But on 13 February 1977, in a television interview, she agreed that along with other members of the Downing Street staff she had put names forward for Mr Wilson's consideration. Obviously determined to keep the row alive together with interest in the sales of his book, Mr Haines went on *Panorama* the next night to allege that Lady Falkender had even influenced the appointment of Cabinet ministers, but when asked by Mr Robin Day for an example, he declined to give one.

Even Sir Harold's denial that delay in publishing his resignation honours list had been occasioned because the Political Honours Scrutiny Committee had raised objections to three of the names on it refused to lie flat. On 27 May 1977, Lady Summerskill, the Labour Party's representative on the committee, wrote a letter to *The Times* to say that the committee "could not approve of at least half the list", and that she and the chairman, the late Lord Crathorne, had expressed themselves so strongly on the subject that they had been astonished to find that with one exception the list had been published unchanged. Commenting in *The Times*, Mr Peter Hennessy cited the missing name as that of Mr Astaire. Lady Summerskill recalled meeting on 5 April with Lord Crathorne, but without the third member of the committee, the Liberal peer Lord Rea, to inspect Sir Harold's list, which indicates that the list had been drawn up within three weeks. The reason it was not published for another seven weeks became clear when Lady Summerskill went on to disclose that she and Lord Crathorne were "both astonished when we read the list of proposed honours. We told the civil servant present that we could not approve of at least half of the list, and would he see that this was conveyed to the Prime Minister. Our only other resort was to ask the Queen to intervene and we felt, at this stage, that this would have been highly injurious to these people".

Confusion seems to have existed as to whether in fact a prime minister's resignation list, as opposed to a dissolution list, should be regarded as an occasion for distributing political honours, when it would automatically become the concern of the Political Honours Scrutiny Committee, or whether it should be seen as a purely personal way for a retiring prime minister to reward friends for personal services — or, indeed, whether it may legitimately be used for both purposes. The committee on this occasion seems to have taken the view that half the names on Sir Harold's list could not be construed as political honours and therefore were none of their business, falling outside the committee's terms of reference. What the whole messy business proved was just how uncertain the committee felt about its actual powers of veto and therefore how impotent it was to act with any constructive effect. Writing a letter to *The Times,* the effect of which could only be to stir up feelings of animosity towards a former prime minister and acutely embarrass almost everyone the Queen had been asked by him to honour, was nothing more than a method of exonerating the committee. Some criticism was levelled at Mr Callaghan for sending the list to Buckingham Palace unchanged, but as he rightly pointed out, in this instance he was merely a post-box; he was in fact in exactly the same position as Lord Rosebery had been when landed with Gladstone's controversial resignation honours list of 1895. It is definitely not the responsibility of an incoming prime minister to query his predecessor's resignation list, lest he has his own queried at a future date.

It was also suggested that the Queen might have raised the matter of the list with Mr Callaghan, but that too would have been quite improper; she could only have raised it with Sir Harold, which indeed the *Guardian,* on 29 May, claimed she had done and without success. The extent, if any, to which the Palace raised objections will not be revealed until the Queen's private papers are lodged in the Royal Archives at Windsor Castle, and then only if any relevant papers are made available after her death to her official biographer, but the passing of seven weeks between the committee meeting on 5 April and publication of the list, taken in conjunction with Lady Summerskill's letter, quite clearly indicates that discussion did take place about the list, and only three parties could have been involved, Sir Harold Wilson (who was almost certainly persuaded to go back to some of the proposed recipients), the Political Honours Scrutiny Committee and the Queen or her private secretary.

In the *Daily Express* on 31 May, the columnist William

Who Gets What...

Hickey wrote that intervention by the Earl of Longford had succeeded in reducing James Goldsmith's honour from a peerage to a knighthood. Lord Longford was quoted as saying, "I did take a certain interest in the matter. It involved contact, but I am not going to say who I contacted." As a Knight of the Garter and a Privy Councillor, Lord Longford could have requested, and would certainly have been granted, an audience with the Queen, or he could have written a letter to her private secretary which would without doubt have been placed before her personally. It seems most unlikely that a telephone call from Lord Longford to Harold Wilson would have cut much ice. Nor surely would an approach from Lord Longford to a member of the Political Honours Scrutiny Committee, who had already sent their comments on the list to the prime minister and who do not care to be lobbied. The Queen and Sir Harold were the only two people it would have been worth Lord Longford's while contacting, and the most probable possibility is that Goldsmith lost a peerage through direct intervention by Lord Longford with the Queen. It would still have been necessary for the Queen to persuade Wilson to alter his proposals, but their relationship was always cordial, and seemingly he agreed. Certainly a manoeuvre by a self-appointed protector of public morals would have accounted for so much delay.

One result of the row over Sir Harold's resignation list was that in May 1977 a number of senior Tories suggested to Mrs Thatcher that in future no prime minister should be allowed to nominate life peers in their personal lists. As Mrs Thatcher has yet to resign or be defeated in a general election, the outcome of that suggestion remains to be tested.

CHAPTER EIGHT

... and How

If one knows how to use a knife and fork and has a title one will never go hungry.
         The 35th Lord Kingsale, premier baron of Ireland
                        and currently a silage pit-builder.

A good deal of the actual mechanical functioning of the honours system is an area of national and public life which those who run it either professionally or in a part-time capacity do their best to keep shrouded in secrecy. They do so in the name of discretion, and to try to protect members of committees through which nominations for honours are filtered from the danger of being lobbied.

There are five sources from which the final honours lists emerge: the Foreign and Commonwealth Office, the Ministry of Defence, the prime ministers or governors of those Commonwealth countries which wish to submit names, the prime minister of the United Kingdom, and the Queen herself, whose personal list consists of those subjects she wishes to honour within the Royal Victorian Order. The Foreign Secretary is responsible for nominations from within the Foreign Office. The Secretary of State for Defence submits names from the three armed services. And within the prime minister's list fall honours to civil servants.

The prime minister is at liberty to place any name she likes on her list, and to knock off any name she dislikes that may have been sent to her as a recommendation, and the extent to which any prime minister takes a personal interest in names on his or her list will inevitably reflect to some extent their particular interest in any special field of activity. Encouraging entrepreneurial initiative might fall into this category, but it can backfire, when someone who has been honoured for his swashbuckling approach to free enterprise, for example, then crashes and leaves a pile of unsecured debts in his wake. Blunders can occur on the arts side as well. Harold Macmillan, a publisher and a civilized man of letters, offered a CBE to Sir Osbert Sitwell, only to receive a well-earned rebuke from Peter Simple in the *Daily Telegraph,* who asked what we were to think of a prime minister who offered a Sitwell a CBE, and what we were to think of a Sitwell who accepted it. Twelve months later, Macmillan made amends by giving Sitwell the CH.

Clearly, however, no modern prime minister has the time or inclination, now that the distribution of honours is so far-flung, to compose personally more than a minute proportion of the Downing Street list, and for the bulk of this purpose a series of committees exist, covering virtually every area of national life: science, medicine, sport, education, commerce, the social services, agriculture, industry, the police, the health service, local government, the Manpower Services Commission and the arts and learning — looked after by the Maecenas Committee. It is the composition, not to mention the conversations, even the existence, of these committees which is the most closely guarded secret concerning the distribution of honours. In fact, as one might expect, senior civil servants sit on committees dealing with industry and local services, while distinguished outsiders, knowledgeable in their own field, are recruited to committees dealing with such specialized subjects as science, medicine and the arts.

At the apex of this pile of committees presides a senior civil servant, the Ceremonial Officer, currently Mrs Mary Hedley-Miller, the first woman ever to hold the post. From her room in the Cabinet Office in Great George Street, overlooking St James's Park, and with the aid of a small full-time secretariat,

...and How

she collates recommendations from the committees and advises them as to the approximate allocation of honours available for recommendation by them and the general shape and shade of the list to which the incumbent prime minister aspires. She also sifts personally between 700 and 800 recommendations sent in each year by members of the public, a stack of letters that represents about a third of all the recommendations received from any source. Having composed a list for the prime minister to consider, Mrs Hedley-Miller sends it first for perusal to the Joint Head of the Home Civil Service, who is also secretary to the Cabinet, at present Sir Robert Armstrong.

Mrs Hedley-Miller (who is already a CBE and can fairly confidently look forward to a DBE by the time she retires) is a very powerful, or at any rate influential, lady. No name is likely to get on to the prime minister's list without her approval, almost any name would be taken off before the list went to the prime minister if she argued strongly enough against it, and her advice, based almost inevitably upon an arbitrary set of criteria, as to who should get a knighthood and who a peerage, who an OBE and who a CBE, is crucial. Her function, if only in an advisory capacity to the web of committees (she also acts as secretary to the Political Honours Scrutiny Committee), can hardly be underestimated when one considers that about five times as many nominations are received every year as honours are awarded.

In making assessments for awards, two basic criteria come into play: degrees of excellence and creativity, and levels of responsibility. But some strange anomalies seem to creep through. Upon what criteria or comparison of excellence, for example, was Fay Compton made CBE in 1975 and Wendy Hillier DBE? Why is Lord Olivier rated fit for an OM (admittedly a personal matter for the Queen) and Sir John Gielgud only the CH? Why for that matter is Lord Olivier in the House of Lords, where his contribution to debates on the theatre has drawn less than ecstatic houses? One can see the criteria of excellence applied to such literary knights as V.S. Pritchett and Angus Wilson, but why has Dodie Smith, for example, a conscientious craftsman and dispenser of innocent pleasure to millions, the export of whose books must have reaped a fortune for the Treasury, received no recognition at all? When Naomi Mitchison, in the 1985 New Year Honours List, received the CBE at the age of 87, and after writing more than seventy books and plays, one was entitled to wonder to what even greater age and productivity did such a distinguished woman of letters have to aspire to receive the DBE?

No special committee deals with the civil service, whose interests are watched over by a steering committee chaired by Sir Robert Armstrong and made up of permanent secretaries. In many ways their work is routine, involved as it is with dishing out awards on a rota system, according to seniority and length of service. One of the most influential committees, with an overall bearing on the whole honours system, is the Higher Honours and Awards Committee, who every five years review the entire allocation within each order of awards to the Bath, St Michael & St George and the British Empire (which at the present time probably contains 100,000 members living). The current size of the Foreign and Commonwealth Office and the Armed Services are factors always taken into account, and any recommendations made by this committee go direct to the Queen.

Anyone can be nominated for an honour, and anybody can make a recommendation. In theory, you can even nominate yourself. All you have to do is write to the Ceremonial Officer, mentioning that Mrs Dora Sludgeface of Tooting Bec has been slaving away for fifty years as matron of an old folks' home and suggesting that an MBE would not come amiss. You will certainly receive a brief acknowledgement, and you may be asked to expand on Mrs Sludgeface's merits, bearing in mind that the country seems to be awash with people doing good, usually in the course of a job for which they are being paid. Further discreet enquiries, especially about someone of whom the Ceremonial Officer has no direct knowledge, may well be made, through area health authorities, the Preparatory Schools Association, absolutely any relevant organization.

Lords-Lieutenant are expected to keep an eye open for

possible worthy recipients of honours in the provinces, and to report on people who have been recommended from their county. It is confidently asserted that the eminence of a person making a recommendation carries no weight whatever; in other words, when the Archbishop of Canterbury recommended, as presumably he did, his personal attendant Mr Terry Waite for an MBE, Mr Waite's chances were no greater than had the recommendation come from the porter at Lambeth Palace. It seems hard to believe, but those in a unique position to know are adamant that it is so, just as they claim that a vast volume of recommendations for a particular person are no more likely to carry the day than a single letter. Occasionally a wife will write, extolling the virtues of her husband, and saying how cross he would be if he knew she had written (which indeed he would, if he knew his way around the world in the slightest degree), and those unsophisticated enough quite blatantly to recommend themselves are politely shown the door. By the time enquiries have been made, anyone trying to sneak an honour by getting his friend Tony to write on his behalf will almost certainly be rumbled.

Whether, despite King George V's positive assertion in 1922 that he would not countenance approaches by members of the Royal Family on behalf of those they thought worthy of an honour, anyone closely connected today with work in which the Royal Family is interested has a more than average chance of receiving an honour must remain open to speculation. Even if members of the Royal Family refrain from mentioning a name to the Queen, for the simple reason that the Queen herself does not make recommendations to the prime minister, there seems to be no reason in principle why they should not drop a line to the Ceremonial Officer just like anyone else. For example, the connection, by no means an improper one, between the knight bachelorhood awarded in the 1985 New Year Honours List to Mr John Cumber, director-general of the Save the Children Fund, and the passionate and personal interest taken in the Fund's work by Princess Anne, could well have been more than coincidental.

Once the prime minister's list has been filtered through the various representative committees to the Ceremonial Officer, and she has formulated her own views before sending the list for approval to the Head of the Civil Service, it lands on the prime minister's desk. The prime minister is unlikely to read every name; most of them will mean nothing to her. But she will almost certainly ask one of her secretaries to read the entire list carefully and to report back. She may easily take a name out or add some nominations of her own, including her own political appointees, those backbenchers she wishes to keep happy with a knighthood or membership of the privy council or anyone she has in mind to send to the House of Lords. These names go to the Political Honours Scrutiny Committee.

The committee always consists of three privy councillors (they need not be peers, but at present they are), who are not, however, members of the government, and by tradition they belong to different parties. The prime minister appoints them entirely on his or her own initiative, and no length of service is specified. It is up to incoming prime ministers to reappoint someone else's nominees (Mrs Thatcher was perfectly happy to keep on Mr Callaghan's selection) or to make new appointments of their own. The present members are all life peers: Lord Shackleton, formally Labour leader in the House of Lords, who acts as chairman, Lord Carr, Tory Home Secretary from 1972-4, and Lord Franks, the Liberal philosopher and academic, who served as British Ambassador to Washington from 1948-52. There is no Social Democratic representative. Lord Shackleton (like his father) is a distinguished explorer, at one time a Labour MP, a Knight of the Garter and formally a director of Rio Tinto Zinc. Lord Franks's career has brought him a string of honours ranging from a humble CBE in 1942 to a KCB, GCMG and the Order of Merit. Lord Carr, who alone of the three does not own up in *Who's Who* to being a member of the committee, brings to the deliberations of the triumvirate, in addition to first-hand experience of political life, a wide-ranging knowledge of industry.

The duties of the committee do not extend to selecting

candidates for honours or recommending what honour they should receive; they act in a purely advisory capacity to the prime minister, and their job is to report whether, after making "such enquiry as they think fit", those nominated for a political honour are "fit and proper persons", taking into account "past history or general character". They regard as "political honours" all those nominations which have not emerged "through the machine", in other words, nominations on the prime minister's list for peerages and knighthoods placed there by the prime minister personally in order to reward someone in his or her own party for services rendered, or to strengthen the party's representation in the House of Lords, or names submitted for the same purpose by the leader of an opposition party, at the invitation of the prime minister.

The committee's terms of reference have been set out in an Order in Council made in 1979. Each nomination for a political honour due to be scrutinized must be accompanied by a statement from the prime minister outlining the services allegedly performed and her reasons for the recommendation, the name and address of the person considered by the prime minister to be responsible for the original recommendation and, most important of all, a "statement by the accredited representative of the prime minister for the purpose that he has made all necessary enquiries and has satisfied himself that no payment, or expectation of payment, to any party or political fund is directly or indirectly associated with the recommendation".

This clear and unambiguous injunction precisely reflects the Prevention of Abuses Act under which Maundy Gregory was prosecuted. Yet its strictly literal observance is openly flaunted, for while the present committee would look with serious suspicion upon someone who appeared to have done nothing to deserve an honour except contribute financially to a political party, they do not regard such a contribution as a bar in itself. They consider their duty discharged by requesting from the prime minister a certificate assuring them that money alone is not the excuse for granting a political honour, and this continues to allow prime ministers a good deal of leeway. The

The Honours System

argument for this line of thought, supported by the leader of the Liberal Party, who has not always seen eye to eye with the committee, is that a person should not be automatically debarred from a life peerage simply for having made a contribution to party funds. Had this been the case, clearly Lord Beaumont of Whitley, a generous benefactor to his party as to so many other causes, and one of the Liberal Party's most able and conscientious life peers, would have been lost to the Upper House.

Left unresolved in some people's minds is the question whether all peerages are or ought to be considered as political honours, especially now that hereditary peerages have been restored. Certainly not all the objections to Mr Wilson's resignation honours list were based on financial grounds; sheer unsuitability alone seems, on this occasion, to have left the old committee unsure how far it could go in advising against certain recommendations, and the whole matter of the "general character of the person" suggests a set of criteria which have nothing necessarily to do with money. The one thing no longer in doubt, at any rate since the 1979 Order in Council was drafted, is that in the event of the committee reporting against a name, and the prime minister determining still to recommend, a copy of the committee's report is to be submitted to the Queen.

No institution could be more British than the Political Honours Scrutiny Committee. Three men (or women) of implacably opposed political views, chosen by the prime minister alone, meet informally, in the utmost cordiality, with no fixed quorum and a chairmanship which seems to have evolved by mutual consent and does not even rotate, in order to scrutinize the credentials of new members of the Upper House of Parliament. When a government reshuffle occurs, for example, and in the interests of political expediency the prime minister deems it desirable at a moment's notice to dispatch to the House of Lords a political colleague of long-standing and eminent respectability like William Whitelaw, even the pleasure of a chat over the port is foregone, and the three wise men simply nod approval over the telephone.

...and How

The question now arises as to what happens after approval of political honours has been indicated by the Scrutiny Committee. There is no question that all non-political honours are submitted to the Queen before the potential recipients are contacted, but it seems that despite King George V's reminder to Ramsay MacDonald that before anyone was offered an honour the king's approval should be obtained, "until which time the individual in question should not be approached on the subject", those being offered a peerage are almost always sounded out by the prime minister before the list goes to the Palace, presumably on the grounds that the Queen has no wish to peruse a list of backbench MPs only to discover later that half of them have no desire to vacate their seat. This is not a new departure. In 1944 Harold Nicolson, at that time an MP, was openly discussing with his friends an offer of a peerage he had received from Anthony Eden, presumably empowered by Churchill to sound him out. In the event, Nicolson decided to remain in the House of Commons. It seems extremely unlikely that King George VI knew anything of Nicolson's ruminations, which were to break out again in 1945, when he told James Lees-Milnes "in strict confidence" that the Labour government wanted to make him a peer and that Attlee had spoken to him about it.[1] Today the clubs of Pall Mall are alive with stories of peers who were telephoned in the bath or while presenting some learned dissertation to an international seminar in Outer Mongolia, to see how they felt about a peerage. According to one Labour member of the House of Lords about as close to the centre of national life as you can get, no one has ever refused, but so far as members of the Liberal Party are concerned, this is certainly not the case.

When the prime minister's list is in final shape, it goes to the Queen, and once she has given her approval, about six weeks before an honours list is due to be published letters are sent from 10 Downing Street signed by the prime minister's principal private secretary (currently Mr F.E.R. Butler), and marked, as are most letters from Downing Street, "In

1. *Prophesying Peace* by James Lees-Milne (London, Chatto and Windus, 1977).

The Honours System

Confidence". "Sir" or "Madam", the letter begins, "The Prime Minister has asked me to inform you, in strict confidence, that she has it in mind, on the occasion of the forthcoming list of [New Year Honours or Birthday Honours], to submit your name to the Queen with a recommendation that Her Majesty may be graciously pleased to approve that you be appointed. . . .

"Before doing so, the Prime Minister would be glad to be assured that this would be agreeable to you. I should be grateful if you would let me know by completing the enclosed form and sending it to me by return of post.

"If you agree that your name should go forward and The Queen accepts the Prime Minister's recommendation, the announcement will be made in the . . . Honours List. You will receive no further communication before the List is published. I am, [Sir or Madam], Your obedient Servant, F. E. R. Butler."

Minor slip-ups occur when this letter, complete with its capital letters for The Queen, goes out; sometimes, for example, Mr Butler seems unclear whether a potential recipient is a married lady or not, but essentially of course the wording of the letter is a fiction, for by the time it is written the prime minister has already obtained the Queen's consent. The expression "in strict confidence" certainly implies that no word of the honour should be whispered, even to one's nearest and dearest, before the honours list is published, and indeed it is astonishing how seldom, if ever, a leak occurs. Most people seem only too happy to sit tight on their secret until around New Year's Day or the Queen's Official Birthday it bursts upon an astonished world. It may be assumed that most husbands receiving an honour involving a title will already know their wife's attitude to one day becoming Lady Blank, although some husbands presumably consult their wives before accepting a peerage or a knighthood; others wait to see the look on her face when she opens *The Times*. About 1.05 per cent of all those offered an honour decline, sometimes out of genuine modesty, sometimes out of political or social conviction. A Jehovah's Witness will always refuse, and a Quaker may, if a title is attached to the honour, for Quakers do not even approve the prefix Mr or Mrs. Things do not, however, always go according to plan. In 1975 a knighthood was announced in the Hong Kong list for Mr Michael Herries, a retired British businessman, who naturally received sackfuls of congratulatory telegrams. What he had never received was a letter offering the honour. The matter was happily put right, apologies were offered and the knighthood accepted.

Compiling an honours list inevitably involves the manufacture of insignia and medals. These days the entire cost falls on the Treasury; there is no charge to recipients for insignia. Much of the routine work is undertaken by the Royal Mint, but some of the more complex and time-consuming enamelling of collars and Stars is farmed out to half a dozen private jewellers. Responsibility for a permanent supply of ribbons, medals, Stars, collars and Badges, as with much else connected with the honours system, rests with the secretary of the Central Chancery of the Orders of Knighthood, at present Major-General Desmond Rice, whose offices are housed in St James's Palace. He is a member of the Queen's Household. Membership of the Orders of Knighthood confer various privileges; marriages, Christenings and memorial services, for example, may be held in the various chapels of the orders and, with the exception of St George's Chapel, Windsor, these are arranged through the secretary of the Central Chancery. He is responsible too for publishing honours in the *London Gazette*, for recording changes of address of recipients of honours, supplying when possible the answers to enquiries about family history, and replacing insignia lost, as often as not through burglary. Each order of chivalry has a service, usually at Westminster Abbey or St Paul's Cathedral, held at varying intervals and attended almost invariably by royalty, and these the chancery is also responsible for organizing.

With the exception of an annual investiture in Edinburgh in the summer, for Scottish recipients of honours, held while the Queen is in residence at the Palace of Holyroodhouse, investitures are normally held on a Tuesday at Buckingham Palace, and there are six in the spring, two in July and another six in the autumn. Only absence abroad or ill health ever

The Honours System

prevents the Queen from holding an investiture herself, and when it is necessary for another member of the Royal Family to deputize, letters patent and a Warrant have to be issued. Those most likely to deputize, providing they are available, are Queen Elizabeth the Queen Mother and the Prince of Wales. Princess Margaret and the Duke of Kent, however, have also held investitures.

Anyone being admitted to the Garter, Thistle, Order of Merit or Companionship of Honour is received in private audience, as are judges when automatically knighted on their promotion to the High Court, and their invitation comes from the Queen's private secretary. The Queen also likes to confer posthumous awards for bravery in private. All other invitations are sent out from the Central Chancery. In order to relieve pressure on the Palace slightly, those awarded the British Empire Medal and the Imperial Service Medal receive these from a Minister, a senior civil servant or a Lord-Lieutenant. Those who are too infirm to attend an investiture — as was Ivy Compton-Burnett in 1967, when she was advanced from CBE to DBE at the absurdly advanced age of 83 — may be presented with their insignia at home by a representative of the Queen. But everyone else save peers goes to the Palace, and in order to have some idea how to behave, a stencilled letter is sent to them from General Rice.

"Sir" or "Madam", he says: "I am commanded to inform you that an Investiture will be held at Buckingham Palace on . . ., at which your attendance is requested.

"I am desired to say that you should arrive at the Palace between the hours of 10 o'clock and 10.30 am [investitures are held at 11 am] and this letter should be shown on entering the gates of the Palace and at the Grand Hall Entrance of the Palace, as no other card of admission is issued to recipients. Cars may be parked in the inner Quadrangle of the Palace under police direction. No windscreen tickets are issued.

"If desired, two guests are permitted to accompany you to watch the Ceremony, and tickets for them may be obtained by making application on the form enclosed herewith [a form asking not only for the guests' names but their relationship to the recipient and their occupation] which should be returned to me as soon as possible."

There then follows a paragraph of forbidding mien, heavily underlined in red ink. "The only exception to this rule," it reads, "is that, if a recipient wishes to bring with [her or him, her or his husband or wife] and two sons, or two daughters, or a son and daughter, a third ticket will be issued, but in NO circumstances will a fourth ticket be issued."

Instructions follow on dress to be worn, which boils down to uniform if appropriate (without orders, decorations or medals, only ribbons, and so far as men are concerned, no swords), morning dress or lounge suit, or, for women, day dress with a hat. Gloves are optional, though what is not permitted is one glove on and one glove off. Recipients can claim travel expenses for themselves but not for their guests. It is forbidden to take cameras into the Palace.

All that peers receive are their letters patent through the post, and no new peer can assume a title until it has been approved and gazetted, which did not, however, prevent *The Times*, only five days after it had been announced in the 1985 New Year Honours List that a former trade-union leader, Mr Frank Chapple, was to be made a Life Peer, from presuming to style him Lord Chapple, which he was not and might never have chosen to become. Indeed, a peer is at liberty to take almost any name providing it is not already in use, or in abeyance, or unless given permission to differentiate by the permanent use of a territorial designation. There is, for example, a nineteenth-century earldom of Russell; hence in 1919 the 1st Baron Russell became Lord Russell of Liverpool, and in 1975 a second barony of Russell was conferred upon a Lord of Appeal in the name of Lord Russell of Killowen. A husband and wife who were both made Life Peers rather neatly retained a joint nomenclature by electing to become Lord Stewart of Fulham and Lady Stewart of Alvechurch. At one time a new knight was debarred from assuming his title until he had received the accolade, but today he may do so as soon as the award has been announced.

The Honours System

At Holyroodhouse investitures take place in the Throne Room, and at Buckingham Palace in the Ball Room, where an orchestra from the Foot Guards plays throughout, to soothe the nerves of everyone except the Queen, and the Royal Household, who conduct themselves as always with cool and calm precision, first ensuring that everyone knows where to locate the delightfully old-fashioned mahogany lavatories (the elderly mother of a distinguished novelist once found it necessary to slip out of the Ball Room, only to be regaled by a solicitous gentleman usher with a glass of water). They then gather into line those to be received, pinning on their costumes a holder for their decoration to be attached to. The vital operation of making certain that the right name is called and the appropriate insignia is instantly to hand is the province of the secretary of the Central Chancery, who places the medals, decorations and insignia on a cushion held by an equerry. A few of those being invested, like actors and senior diplomats, will be known to the Queen, but it is impossible for her to be briefed on all the recipients, to whom she nevertheless always manages to say a few words as she bestows her honours at an approximate rate of two per minute. The conversations, however, tend to be a little stilted.

"What do you do?" the Queen will ask.

"I write books, Ma'am."

"Oh, you're a writer."

The recipient bows or curtsies before and after being invested, having been instructed beforehand in the niceties of court etiquette, and on retiring they have their insignia taken off them and placed in a box, after which they return to the Ball Room to sit with their guests.

It was unfortunate for Doris Speed, the actress who for many years played Annie Walker in the television series *Coronation Street*, that by the time she went to the Palace to receive an MBE in 1977 she had become a little deaf and therefore failed to catch what the Queen said to her. "You can't really ask her to speak up," she commented afterwards, adding that she thought the Queen was "a very sweet person" who had given her a charming smile. "I must say," Miss Speed reported to the press waiting outside the Palace, "as one professional to another she has a most gruelling job meeting all these people."

It is literally the dream of millions of the Queen's subjects to be one of those she meets, as often as not for tea.[2] For many others, an investiture will suffice, very possibly because the act of accepting an honour is tantamount to swearing an oath of allegiance, of being invited to cement that relationship between the recipient of an honour and the fountain of honour which enshrines a monarchal nation's attitude to its monarchy and to itself, fulfilling a wish to live and shine within the reflected glory of the monarch. If Great Britain became a republic, an honours system could still exist, but without the Queen and the Ball Room, the debonair members of the Household, the fabulous china in glass cases, the baroque and gilt, the sense of having wandered into the home of someone who is better off than you but really just the same, it would all be seen as far less fun and far less glamorous, and therefore less worth bothering to maintain, less an occasion for a slap-up lunch afterwards, and far less unreal, part of that seemingly necessary fantasy world of pantomines and soap opera. Whether the demise of the honours system as we know it today would be inherently a good or a bad thing is another matter.

---

2. *Dreams About H.M. the Queen,* collected and interpreted by Brian Masters (London, Blond & Briggs, 1972).

CHAPTER NINE
Conclusions

I am a friend to subordination, as most conducive to the happiness of society. There is a reciprocal pleasure in governing and being governed. . . . Subordination tends greatly to human happiness. Were we all upon an equality we should have no other enjoyment than mere animal pleasure. . . . I would no more deprive a nobleman of his rank, than of his money.

Dr Johnson.

"Honours are useful and harmless, and they arouse severe indignation only among those who make the mistake of treating them too seriously," *The Times* informed the world on 27 November 1979. There are many who would agree with this; there are others who would agree only in part. Honours may well be useful but not necessarily harmless, for it can be argued that some honours, by the very nature of their class structure, are socially devisive, while others, like hereditary peerages that automatically confer a seat in Parliament, are demonstratively undemocratic. There is also, of course, no law against taking the honours system too seriously, or even seriously, and anybody who wishes to sweep away the entire edifice would be perfectly entitled to their ambition; their difficulty might be in drafting effective legislation, or merely in altering social usage, for unless a man or woman intends to defraud he or she is perfectly at liberty in law to call themselves

Lord Luvaduck or Lady Littlehampton, and republics on the continent abound with princes, counts and barons left over from their days as monarchies. And anybody is free to give a present, so that even if an attempt was made to abolish the honours system formally there would be nothing to prevent the sovereign from handing to anyone he or she chose a nicely gift-wrapped parcel containing a chunk of metal that just happened to have "For Merit" engraved on it. One only needs to attend the annual dinner of the Monarchist League to feast one's eyes on the cardboard stars and badges still dished out by exiled royalty to their fervant, sometimes rather dotty, admirers.

But in fact, no serious person, and certainly no political party, has ever contemplated abolishing the entire system, although in recent years the Labour Party has come very close to it. In 1981 they produced a policy document suggesting the abolition of peerages, baronetcies and knighthoods in the United Kingdom, while leaving it open for Commonwealth countries to continue to nominate for honours if they so wished; the document also advocated the substitution of two basic awards, one for gallantry and one for "conspicuous service to the community", for the present range of lesser honours, but it was less than specific about what to do with regard to awards at present in the personal gift of the sovereign, and of the continued creation of royal dukedoms. And although not committed to abolishing existing titles, the Labour Party has called for the abolition of the House of Lords. Until that happy day, the present leader of the party, Mr Neil Kinnock, is to continue to put forward names for working peers "as and when necessary", but for some strange reason, for inclusion only in the new year honours lists, not in the Queen's birthday lists. He is against knighthoods by way of political honours, but wants to be asked to nominate awards for community service. Not only does he support the 1983 party manifesto's call to "abolish the undemocratic House of Lords as quickly as possible" but he is in favour of a one-chamber parliament, believing apparently that it would be possible to reform the House of Commons so as to turn it into an efficient watch-dog over itself.

The leader of the Social Democrats, Dr David Owen, has no time for automatic awards to civil servants, diplomats and service chiefs on the grounds of long service and good conduct, and he believes that the only area of what he calls "pure party political patronage" should relate to the nomination of life members of the House of Lords — but only until such time as the second chamber has been reformed so as to contain "an elected element where nominated members would be chosen by an independent commission". The leader of the Liberal Party, Mr David Steel, on the other hand, has no objection in principle to political honours, on the grounds that service to a political party is as much a service to the country as any other activity singled out for acknowledgement in the honours lists; there is, he believes, no grounds for excluding from the honours system those who serve the democratic process. But he regards the present allocation of honours to his own party as "miserly" (in the New Year Honours List for 1985 members of the Liberal Party received five awards for political services), and he is anxious to continue nominating party workers on as broad a geographical basis as possible. He does not regard a life peerage bestowed on a "working peer", someone like Lord Ezra, as an honour, and despite the comparatively rare occasions when he has been invited to nominate working peers, Mr. Steel has found himself in opposition to the Political Honours Scrutiny Comitee, once over his nomination of someone who many years before had committed a very minor offence; he argued the person's case, and lost.

Although in 1978 a Conservative Party committee under the chairmanship of Lord Home recommended a second chamber composed partly of elected and partly of nominated members, the Conservative Party under Mrs Thatcher's leadership remains perfectly content with the continued creation of life peers under the sole patronage of the prime minister, together with the perpetuation of a hereditary element within the House of Lords. With the Labour Party committed to abolishing the second chamber, only the Liberal Party and the

Social Democratic Party, working within their Alliance, have given serious consideration in recent times to reform of the House of Lords, producing a report in August 1983 which affirms their belief in the necessity for a second chamber, to act "as a check on the power of a government holding a majority in the House of Commons to force through legislation". They renounce both the hereditary principle and political patronage as methods of filling a second chamber, and recommend instead, as Lord Home's committee did, a chamber composed partly of elected and partly of nominated members. Those who would nominate would be a Standing Commission consisting mainly of senior privy councillors, and they feel that selections should, over the years, be kept in rough balance with the current strengths of the political parties in the country. They want to see members of the chamber drawn from "all sections of the community and from important areas of national life". Any existing peer not elected by the Standing Commission would cease to be a member of whatever forum the new chamber was called (and presumably any peer would then be eligible to stand for election to the House of Commons). They feel that the automatic inclusion of a fixed number of Anglican bishops would be inappropriate (it may be assumed that the Standing Commission would be free to nominate bishops, however), and that no Lords of Appeal in Ordinary should sit, the final court of appeal becoming the Judicial Committee of the Privy Council. Members of the new chamber would be appointed for a period of ten years, be eligible for reappointment, and free to resign at any time.

The course of modern legislative programmes and their handling in both Houses of Parliament does seem to reinforce the value and desirability of a scrutinizing second chamber, independent of the Commons and with the time and experience to examine in detail controversial and complicated legislation. In one recent session the Lords, despite the overwhelming Conservative majority in the House of Commons and their own powerfully built-in Conservative supremacy, voted down no fewer than forty-six government measures. The serious attention they pay to the nation's affairs

Conclusions

may also be reflected in the fact that in 1945 the Lords dealt with 68 written questions, in 1983 with 1,982. Credit for the conduct of the House of Lords cannot, of course, necessarily be attributed to its present composition; when necessary, backwoodsmen are still rounded up in a most unseemly way, but sometimes with rather comic results. In a desperate attempt to defeat the government in June 1984 over its plans to abolish the Greater London Council, the Liberals managed to whip up the 3rd and 74-year-old Lord De Ramsey, a peer, but not a very active one in political terms, since the age of 15, only to discover that his incipient Liberal sentiments had been overtaken by a latent ambition to vote against Ken Livingstone, leader of the GLC, with the result that he went into the government lobby.

The peerage came into existence as a bulwark around which to shield and defend the monarchy and as a means of providing continuity in government before the evolution of parliamentary democracy. As a constituent of government, it must surely now be said that the peerage is an anachronism, for in a social democracy the concept of a hereditary right to rule is quite simply indefensible. In this respect there is no analogy between a hereditary peerage and a hereditary monarchy, for the monarch no longer enacts or declines to sanction Acts of Parliament. Indeed, it is even questionable whether today a constitutional monarchy is socially dependent upon the existence of a hereditary peerage, and in the unlikely event of both the House of Lords and the peerage being abolished, the Crown could still continue to exercise a constitutional function and to draw (as it does already) enough support and loyalty from commoners to ensure its survival.

No matter how good a job the House of Lords as at present constituted may be said to be doing by way of scrutinizing legislation (and most professional political commentators seem to be agreed that it is doing a remarkably good job), if the hereditary element still contained in the second chamber is undemocratic and indefensible, that element should go. (Democracy in this context is not just a matter of hereditary peers not being elected; life peers are not, and those members of a reformed second chamber who were nominated by a Standing Commission would not be. The difference is that life peers — as nominated members of a second chamber would be — are appointed by the will of Parliament enshrined in an Act, whereas hereditary peers sit without any authority other than that of the sovereign, frequently now dead, who first summoned their predecessors.) And if hereditary peers are to be barred from membership as of right, the entire reasoning, such as it ever was, for inventing life peers collapses. It would clearly be ridiculous to bar hereditary peers but to admit life peers. The purpose of the life peer, however, in essence the appointment of a senator, need not be scrapped; the recommendations made by the Liberal/SDP Alliance to create a reformed second chamber consisting of both elected and appointed representatives, and especially the proviso that those appointed should no longer be the nominees of the prime minister, are the most sensible currently on offer, and in a democracy that has come of age they ought to find majority support among all those who believe that no House of Commons should ever be left to legislate without safeguards, that a hereditary upper house is really an insult, and that a national forum for debate divorced from the hectic, often ill-tempered and frenetic mêlée of party politics is a highly desirable and beneficial adjunct to the Commons.

If hereditary membership of the House of Lords is abolished, the prime purpose of creating hereditary peers disappears. The only reason remaining for their creation would be to perpetuate a famous name, and in so doing to confer titles, dignity and privileges upon men and women as yet unborn. It seems with hindsight that the name of John Churchill, Duke of Marlborough, would have remained no less firmly implanted in the minds and memories of schoolboys and historians alike had he remained John Churchill, or been the one and only duke of Marlborough; the existence of a Duke of Marlborough today cannot conceivably do anything to enhance the deeds of his famous ancestor. In other words, it has really always been humbug to imagine that a hereditary peerage was required for this purpose. Would anybody be likely to forget the life and times of Lord Mountbatten if his daughter was not Lady Mountbatten?

If peers are no longer to be allowed to govern by virtue of being born in a certain bed, there is now no serious argument for creating any new hereditary peers. There are un-serious arguments, of course; that peers, by being sometimes pleasantly eccentric and often very rich, provide much needed glamour and add to the diversity of the nation's social life. This may be so, and thanks to the quirks of history there are still plenty such to fill the bill; but the creation of new ones, as we approach the twenty-first century having already entered the space age, cannot possibly be justified. By the same token, neither could the creation of new baronets. Ever anxious to stem the flow of old blood with injections of new, the Standing Council of the Baronetage have had two meetings with Mrs Thatcher to try to persuade her to reintroduce baronetcies along with hereditary peerages, but seem so far to have failed to carry the argument.

But any suggestion that existing hereditary (or life) peerages or baronetcies should be abolished could not be justified either. The charting of the future is a very different pastime to rewriting history. The peerage as it has developed and been inherited, for better or for worse, contains ineradicable reminders of the nation's social, economic, political and military history; suddenly to try to rub it out in a fit of pique or misplaced egalitarianism would be childish at best and destructive at worst. The peerage is best left to evolve (perhaps eventually to the point of extinction) and to take its chances together with all the other elements in an ever-changing social scene.

It should be added that the very occasional bestowal of hereditary peerages "in special cases" to mark outstanding public service cannot be justified if the general principle of not creating new hereditary peerages is accepted. What Mrs Thatcher in effect did in recommending a somewhat belated earldom for Mr Harold Macmillan, a former prime minister, was to clear the way for a future leader of the Conservative Party eventually to send her to the House of Lords as a countess in her own right, with a title that would one day descend — not too deservingly, one might feel — on her son. And almost deliberately to single out for a hereditary peerage of all things, men believed most unlikely to be going to produce an heir would in itself be a farce. There are plently of other honours available besides peerages with which to garland our national heroes.

If the recommendations of the Liberal/SDP Alliance were accepted, and a Standing Commission were to select a proportion of the members of a reformed second chamber (other members being elected), the question whether to award peerages as political honours would vanish. Remaining would be the question of whether backbenchers and workers for the political parties in the House of Commons and the constituencies should continue to receive knighthoods, CBEs and so on. It has been said that to include in the honours lists pop stars and postmistresses but to exclude politicians would be a public affectation. This is probably correct, and on balance the arguments for and against political honours (excluding peerages) almost certainly come down in favour of retaining them, providing they are distributed openly and above board, and are clearly recognized for what they are, rewards for services to a political party, and hence in some measure to the democratic process. To disguise them as honours for public services would be wrong. What is entirely unsatisfactory at present is the meagre allocation of political honours to those opposition parties in Parliament who wish to nominate for them. Quite obviously they should at the very least reflect the strength of the parties in Parliament, and preferably in the country. At the 1983 general election the Alliance received 25 per cent of the popular vote. Therefore, if the Alliance so wishes, its active party members should receive 25 per cent of the available political honours. Should such an arrangement be seen as some frightful infringement of the prime minister's rights, political patronage should be taken away from her and handed over to the Political Honours Scrutiny Committee, who can hardly be said to be overworked.

Conclusions

Any re-allocation of the great mass of awards announced each year presents more complex problems. As a matter of principle, however, it does not seem that there can be any rational argument for the customary wholesale distribution of honours to civil servants, diplomats and members of the armed forces on grounds of seniority alone. In this respect they are treated uniquely, and without justification. At a certain level of responsibility, at ambassadorial level, for example, it may well be thought advisable, so long as we have an honours system, for the senior representative of the government abroad to go out to dinner with a Broad Ribbon over his shoulder and a Star on his breast. Otherwise, as for everyone else, an award for a civil servant or a colonel or a first secretary should be to mark especial merit. There should be no other criteria. Length of service is the least meritorious factor of all.

Rather than reduce the numbers of those throughout the spectrum of public life who most frequently receive awards within the Order of the British Empire, it has been suggested that the honours system should be expanded, to include a new order for sport, or an order in the name of Queen Elizabeth II. Heaven forbid. There are enough orders already. Those that already exist have irreplaceable and fascinating historical roots and connections, and any move to abandon existing orders in order to replace them with new ones would be even more reprehensible than adding to their numbers. The ubiquitous Order of the British Empire serves perfectly adequately as a general order for the general public. Suggestions that because there is no longer an empire the name should be changed are as ridiculous as it would be to update the Order of the Bath to the Order of the Bidet; the less history is tampered with the better.

There is perhaps one slightly disquieting group of people who not infrequently appear in the honours lists, and have done so now since the turn of the century. These are newspaper proprietors, editors and working journalists. It may be felt that in order to preserve their impartiality and integrity no one connected with newspapers, radio or television should dream of accepting an honour, coming as it inevitably does on the recommendation of the leader of one or other of the political parties. The fact is that newspaper proprietors rarely hide their political allegiance; they openly campaign for the party of their choice, and their awards when they come are not intended to mark the production of well-written newspapers but to thank them for openly supporting a political party. The same is true of most editors and of many working journalists. It cannot seriously be assumed that a majority among the senior editorial members of the staff of the *Daily Mail*, for instance, are socialists. The working journalist who might be thought to be in danger of compromising his impartiality by accepting an honour is someone like Sir Robin Day or Sir Alistair Burnet. It has to be said that over a quarter of a century, Robin Day has consistently proved himself one of the most professional, well-informed and competent interviewers in the political arena (not even turning a hair when Mrs Thatcher, who might have been expected to recall that he had been knighted, referred to him throughout an interview as Mr Day), and not once has he ever compromised his freedom of action or personal or professional integrity. However, many of his fellow journalists would refuse point-blank to accept an honour on the grounds of justice needing to be seen to be done, for the risk of even being thought to be beholden to politicians is one that some members of the profession are just not prepared to run. In an interview in the *Observer* on 18 November 1984, Sir Robin Day, when asked if he had any qualms about his knighthood, had this to say: "Why should I? I don't think journalists are superior mortals, above accepting what other people are perfectly honoured and happy to accept. I have never understood why some journalists are thrilled to bits to be honoured by Granada's *What the Papers Say* and feel that it might be wrong for them to accept an honour given in the name of the Queen." Some may think that a disingenuous answer. The Granada panel of judges, after all, are hardly likely to be interviewed by Sir Robin on some controversial political issue on *The World at One*. Nevertheless it does seem that individual journalists should be left to make their own

Conclusions

personal decision in the matter of honours; to bar them automatically would be fatuous, but no journalist who does accept an honour should be in the least surprised if it causes his or her impartial judgement to be doubted.

A far more serious matter concerns the distribution of awards for gallantry on a blatant class-orientated basis. To retain medals for privates and crosses for officers is frankly obscene. The army's Military Medal and Distinguished Conduct Medal, along with equivalent decorations in the navy and air force, should be abolished and the Military Cross and Distinguished Service Order and their equivalents extended to embrace all ranks. Those existing holders of the MM, DCM and so on should be free to retain them if they wish, or to exchange them for the equivalent commissioned officer's decoration. The retention of a grading system to recognize degrees of bravery is, of course, another matter, and if every soldier, no matter what his rank, was eligible to receive, according to the circumstances and endeavours of his action, the MC, the DSO and the VC we should all know at a glance whom we were honouring and why.

Retention by the sovereign of those orders at present in her personal gift seems perfectly right and proper. The numbers of those receiving the Garter, Thistle and Order of Merit are minimal in relation to the entire honours system, and unless the sovereign can exercise personal prerogative and initiative within at least one private order (the Royal Victorian Order) the stated objective within the constitution, that the sovereign is the fountain of honour, will become a fiction indeed. Prime ministers already exercise far more patronage than is good for them, filling bishoprics and all sorts of other appointments that they know nothing about, and if anyone wields more patronage within the honours system than they should it is the prime minister of the day, not the sovereign.

So far as the choice of recipients is concerned for honours which do not fall within the range of political or semi-automatic awards — people such as writers, actors, sportsmen, police officers, nurses, directors of charities and of banks — everyone will have their personal view and not everyone could ever be wholly satisfied. The most glaring inequality is in the dearth of senior honours for women. It is astonishing how few women in public life receive the CH, a privy councillorship or the DBE for work outside politics but conducted in the national interest for which men become knights bachelor as a matter of course. And so long as life peerages remain in existence, they should be utilized by the prime minister to supplement political appointments to the House of Lords with the really imaginative appointment of men and women whose contributions to debates in the Lords would enhance the prestige of Parliament. Could any woman have been a more suitable choice for a life peerage than Mrs Frances Temple, widow of the wartime archbishop of Canterbury, who died on 18 May 1984 at the age of 93? An immensely competent and compassionate woman, she was a member of the Curtis Committee whose deliberations led to the 1948 Children Act, and she knew and cared far more about the inhabitants of borstals and prisons (including Dartmoor, where she worked among recidivists) than most members of the House of Commons, and even many Home Secretaries. But no one had the sense to offer her a national platform.

There seems also to be a pathetic lack of imagination in awards for bravery in peacetime. In Liverpool, Mrs Pamela Walsh tackled three shotgun raiders single-handed, holding on to one of the raiders even though he struck her twice on the head with the barrel and butt of his gun, fracturing her skull. On 30 May 1984, the Chief Constable of Nottingham told the annual conference of the Chief Police Officer's Association, "Mrs Walsh's resourcefulness and courageous behaviour in tackling three armed and determined robbers is worthy of the highest commendation." She was awarded something called the Provincial Police Gold Medal for Bravery. What, one wonders, is the George Cross supposed to be for?

If you wish to receive an honour from the Queen, what is your best way of going about it? The first and soundest advice you should heed is not to write to the Queen to ask for one. Lie low, but not too low. Bring yourself to the attention of the

Conclusions

Establishment by all means, but preferably by a level-headed application to duty rather than by getting arrested for importuning. The really ambitious boy who is also reasonably clever and yearns for a knighthood will plan his progress in the honours stakes while he is still in the sixth form, by the simple expedient of choosing a career in which he is (as things stand at present) almost bound to succeed. If he goes into the armed forces, the diplomatic service or the civil service, or gets diverted from one of those callings to the Royal Household, and he reaches the top he will almost certainly get a knighthood, maybe even a life peerage. And on the way up he will also receive at least a CBE, a CMG or a CB. A career in politics — although more risky because one's constitutents tend from time to time not to return one to Parliament — is another job to which the youth ambitious for an honour should give careful consideration. But beware of vocations. They tend to be relied upon to supply their own reward. Clergymen and social workers, unless immensely eminent through learning or position, seldom receive an honour, and those engaged in charitable pursuits far outstrip in numbers any annual supply of MBEs. What is often quite useful is to combine an ostentatious application to charitable work with a well publicized job, preferably in broadcasting or on the stage. That way no one can be sure whether you have been honoured for showing off or exercising humility, and if you can raise £1 million by walking on your hands for twenty-five miles while attracting royal patronage your enthusiam may well catch the eye of those whose task it is to brighten the honours lists without cheapening them.

The Conservative backbencher who feels that for his wife's sake a knighthood would be fun is best advised to do nothing and to do it well, voting over twenty-five years the way he is told, answering his constituents' letters by return of post and never taking up a maverick cause. Should an MP find himself in the cabinet, things are bound to go wrong from time to time, and he will have to wait until retirement to the House of Lords enables him to don the cloak of respectability. No matter what kind of a mess he has made of the nation's financial affairs in his fifties, if he survives into his seventies, and preferably his eighties, he will be acclaimed a hero, and almost certainly end up with a peerage and the Order of Merit.

One should never forget that honours do not grow on trees, despite the numbers awarded, and that they are not public property but the gift of the Establishment, who either bestow them on their own kind or upon those of the vulgar mob who tow the establishment line. Had the Beatles sung the sort of songs favoured by George Formby they might never have been given MBEs. No advice is needed for the genuinely modest, philanthropic, altruistic person plucked from provincial obscurity to be adorned with an OBE as an example to others to slog away, perhaps at a boring job or in a good cause, but anyone closer to the secretive and rather self-satisfied clubland that operates the honours system, as it does the running of every aspect of the Establishment, should take especial care not to cross, maybe even at fourth or fifth remove, the paths of certain specific individuals. A careless, seemingly amusing but perhaps rather cutting remark, made at a private dinner party in Henley-on-Thames, given by a stockbroker whose wife happens to play bridge once a month with a woman whose hairdresser has acquired a royal warrant and is now patronized by You-Know-Who from the civil service, could in five years' time surface with disastrous results. Above all else, if you really and truly want to receive an honour, do not, whatever else you do, write a book on the subject.

Sir Winston Churchill, probably the only man in history to have turned down a dukedom but who did become a Knight Companion of the Most Noble Order of the Garter, a Member of the Order of Merit and a Companion of Honour, had this to say about the purpose of the honours system: "The object in presenting medals, stars and ribbons is to give pride and pleasure to those who deserve them." His wartime deputy prime minister, Earl Attlee, commenting in his own modest way on a life of not inconsiderable achievements, perhaps deserves the last word, for doodling one day in retirement he

Conclusions

came up with that hardest achievement of all, the perfect limerick:

> Few thought he was even a starter
> There were many who thought themselves smarter
> But he ended PM
> CH and OM
> An earl and a knight of the garter.

BOOKS CONSULTED INCLUDE:

Battiscombe, Georgina: *Queen Alexandra* (London, Constable, 1969).
British Orders and Awards (London, Kaye & Ward, 1968).
Brooke, John: *King George III* (London, Constable, 1972).
Burke's Peerage, Baronetage and Knightage.
Cullen, Tom: *Maundy Gregory: Purveyor of Honours* (London, The Bodley Head, 1974).
Debrett's Peerage and Baronetage.
De la Bere, Brigadier Sir Ivan: *The Queen's Orders of Chivalry* (London, William Kimber, 1961).
Halsbury's Laws of England (London, Butterworth).
Hankinson, Cyril: *My Forty Years with Debrett* (London, Robert Hale, 1963).
Hibbert, Christopher: *Edward VII* (London, Allen Lane, 1976).
Keen, Maurice: *Chivalry* (New Haven, Yale University Press, 1984).
Lockyer, Roger: *Buckingham: The Life and Political Career of George Villiers, First Duke of Buckingham, 1592-1625* (London, Longman, 1981).
Maitland, F.W.: *The Constitutional History of England* (Cambridge University Press, 1908).
Marquand, David: *Ramsay MacDonald* (London, Jonathan Cape, 1977).
Nicolson, Harold: *King George V: His Life and Reign* (London, Constable, 1952).
Owen, David: *A Future That Will Work* (London, Viking, 1984).
Ponsonby, Sir Frederick: *Recollections of Three Reigns* (London, Eyre & Spottiswoode, 1951).
Reed, Donald: *Edwardian England* (History Book Club, 1972).
Rose, Kenneth: *King George V* (London, Weidenfeld & Nicolson, 1983).
Sampson, Anthony: *Anatomy of Britain* (London, Hodder & Stoughton, 1962).
Stone, Lawrence: *The Crisis of the Aristocracy, 1558-1641* (Oxford University Press, 1965).
Turner, E.S.: *Amazing Grace* (London, Michael Joseph, 1975).
Victorian Studies, Vol.III (Indiana University Press).

Whitaker's Almanack (London).

Wilson, Harold: *The Governance of Britain* (London, Weidenfeld & Nicolson and Michael Joseph, 1976).

Wilson, Harold: *The Labour Government 1964-70: A Personal Record* (London, Weidenfeld & Nicolson and Michael Joseph, 1971).

Index

Abercorn, 5th Duke of, 42
Abercorn, dukedom of, 45
Aberdeen, 7th Earl of (later Marquess of Aberdeen & Temair), 100
Aga Khan, H. H. Sir Sultan Mahomed Shah, The, 126
Airlie, 12th Earl of, 43
Aitken, Sir Max, Bt. (later Lord Beaverbrook), 100
Albany, Count of (the Young Pretender), fn 68
Albany, Countess of, fn 68
Albert Edward, H. R. H. Prince, *see* Clarence & Avondale, Duke of
Albert, H. R. H. the Prince Consort, 47, 51
Alexandra, H. H. Princess, 113
Alexandra of Kent, H. R. H. Princess, 43-4
Alexandra, Queen (formerly Princess of Wales), 47, 58, 65, 67, admitted to Garter, 71; 76, 94, 99, 113, 123
Alfred the Great, King, 21
Alice, H. R. H. Princess, Countess of Athlone, 71
Alice, H. R. H. Princess, Duchess of Gloucester, 44
Allain, Yves, 137
Allenby, 1st Viscount, 25
Andrew, H. R. H. Prince, 43, 47
Anne, H. R. H. Princess, 43-4, 46, 155
Annenberg, Walter, K. B. E., 126
Appellate Jurisdiction Act 1876, 87
Armstrong, Sir Robert, 153-4, 156
Arnold, Sydney, 124
Arthur of Connaught, H. R. H. Princess, 113
Arthur, King, 63
Arundel, Earl of, 35
Ashdown, Lord, 146
Ashton, Sir Frederick, 77
Askew, Arthur, 119
Asquith, Herbert (later Earl of Oxford & Asquith), plans to swamp House of Lords, 95-9; 100, 107, 112, fn 125
Astaire, Jarvis, 145, 147
Astor, 1st Viscount, 113
Athelstan, King, 21
Attlee, Clement (later Earl Attlee), baronetcies, 59; restores Garter to the Crown, 65, and Thistle, 66; 159, 180-1
Avon, 1st Earl of (formerly Sir Anthony Eden), 48, fn 125, 159

Bach, Johann Sebastian, 145
Bacon, Sir Edmund, Bt., 55
Bacon, Sir Francis, 32, 54
Bacon, Sir Nicholas, Bt., 54
Baker, Sir Stanley, 142
Baldwin, Stanley, 123
Balfour, Arthur (later Earl Balfour), 25, 67, Lords Reform, 96; 100
Barons, precedence, 10, 55; 11, purpose, 22, 27; origins, 23, 28, 50; style, 41; creations since Life Peerage Act 1958, 41; numbers, 49
Baronetage, The, origins, 53-4; style, 53; cost, 54-6, 102, 108; first creations, 55; for political services, 57, and other purposes, 59-61; prospects of survival, 60, 173; numbers, 60, 124; missing, 60; incomes, 88; 20th-century creations, 93
Barrie, Sir James, 99
Bartlett, Sir Herbert, Bt., 60
Bath, Order of, 11, 65, origins and development, 69, 86; those eligible, 70; women admitted, 71; 78-9, 86, 112, 127, numbers, 131; 154, 175, 179
Beaconsfield, Viscountess, 86
Beatles, The, 180
Beatrice, H. R. H. Princess (later Princess Henry of Battenberg), 44
Beauchamp de Holt, John (later Lord Kidderminster), 23
Beaufort, 10th Duke of, 48
Beaufort, dukes of, 66
Beaumont, Lord (later Viscount), 23
Beaumont of Whitley, Lord, 158
Bedford, Duke of, 20; and dukes of, 93
Begin, Menachem, 38
Bellairs, the Reverend H. W., 58
Benn, Anthony Wedgwood, 38
Bennett, Thomas, 29-30
Bentinck, Augusta (later Baroness Bolsover), 87
Beresford, Lady Charles, 99
Berkeley, Marquess of, 20
Berners, 10th Baroness, 24
Berners, 9th Lord, 24
Bernhard, H. R. H. Prince of the Netherlands, 58
Bhumibol Adulyadej, King of Thailand, 128

185

The Honours System

Bigge, Sir Arthur (later Lord Stamfordham), 96, 98-101, 109, 112-13, 118, 124-5
Billyard-Leake, Edward, 119, 122
Birkenhead, 1st Earl of, 106, 115
Birkett, Norman, 120
Bishops, 20, 50, 73, 129, 170, 177
Black Prince, The (1st Duke of Cornwall), 26, 106
Blunt, (formerly Sir) Anthony, 64
Bolles, Lady (Mary), Bt., 56
Bonar Law, Richard, 113
Bondfield, Margaret, 83
Bowes-Lyon, Lady Elizabeth, see Elizabeth the Queen Mother
Brandenburg, Margrave of, 27
British Empire Medal, 11, 162
British Empire, Order of, 11, 65, women admitted, 71; instituted, 72; eligibility, 72-3; insignia, 73; 109, numbers, 131-2; 154, 175, 178-80
Brooks, Oliver, V. C., 78
Broughton, Urban H., 25
Buckingham, Duchess of, 56
Buckingham, 1st Duke of, see Villiers, George
Burghley, Lord, 28-9
Burke, Sir Henry Farnham, 80
Burnet, Sir Alistair, 176
Burns, Sir Terence, 139
Butler, the Hon. Adam, 135
Butler, F. E. R., 159-60
Butler, Sir Michael, 133

Caligula, Emperor of Rome, 142
Callaghan, James, 131, 139, 145-6, 148, 156
Campbell-Bannerman, Sir Henry, 114
Canterbury, Archbishop of (Robert Runcie), 155
Canute, King, 23, 50
Cardigan, 7th Earl of, 78
Carlisle, Earl of, 35
Carnock, 1st Lord, 75
Carr, Lord, 156
Carrington, 3rd Lord, 66
Carrington, 6th Lord, 38
Casement, (formerly Sir) Roger, 64
Castlemaine, Lady (later Duchess of Cleveland), 45
Cayzer, Sir William (later Lord Cayzer), 136
Central Chancery of the Orders of Knighthood, The, 12, 68, 161-4
Ceremonial Officer, The, 12, 152-6
Chamberlain, Neville, fn 125
Chamberlayne, Edward, 20
Chapple, Lord, 163
Charles I, 12, 20, bestows Garter on son, 25; sale of honours, 29, 35, 39, 54, 56; 34, creates woman baronet, 56; 57, 68, 95
Charles II, bestows Garter on Charles Lennox, 22; creates duchesses, 26; 35, 45, 57, fn 68
Chivalry, orders of, 11; age of, 63-4, and Sir Galahad, 22, and Sir Launcelot, 93; 73, church services, 161
Churchill, John (1st Duke of Marlborough), 24, 37, 172
Churchill, John, 99
Churchill, Sir Winston, declines dukedom, 46; revives baronetcies, 59; 65, 68, 77, 107-8, fn 125, 159, 180
Cicely, Princess, 43
Clarence & Avondale, H. R. H. the Duke of, 47
Clark, Lord, 76
Clayton, Sir Robert, 136
Clerkship of Enrolments, The, 35
Clinton, Lord, 20
Coggan, Lord (formerly archbishop of Canterbury), 74
Coke, Sir Edward, 20
Companionship of Honour, 11, 40, women admitted, 71; founded 76-7; numbers 77; precedence, 77; 131, 134, 162, 178
Compton, Fay, 153
Compton-Burnett, Dame Ivy, 162
Constitution, The, 21, fn 35, 50, 87, 96, 100, 177
Conway, Viscount, 35
Cooper, Lady Diana, 126
Cornwall, dukedom of, 26
Cotter, Sir James, Bt., 55
Cotton, Sir Robert, 54
Craig, Sir James (later Viscount Craigavon), 101
Cranfield, Lionel, 33
Cranmer, Archbishop Thomas, 21
Crathorne, 1st Lord, 147
Crawford, earldom of, 48
Crewe, Earl of (later Marquess of), 97-8, 100
Cripps, Sir Stafford, 99
Critchley, Julian, 138-9
Croft, Henry, 109
Crome, John, 114
Cromwell, Oliver, fn 35
Crown of India, Order of, founded, 71, 86; women admitted, 71
Cumber, Sir John, 155
Curzon, Marquess, 25, 75

Dalton, Catherine, 73
Dalton, Canon John, 73
Dalyell, Tam, 57
Daventry, Viscountess, 86
Davidson, 1st Viscount, 102
Davies, Ethel, 121
Dawson, Sir Douglas, 80-1
Dawson of Penn, Viscount, 83
Day, (later Sir) Robin, 147, 176
Debrett's, 12, 49, 71, 139
Decorations, 11, and class divisions, 41, 82, 177

186

Index

de Keroualle, Louise Renée de Penancoet (later Duchess of Portsmouth), 45
de la Pole, William (later Duke of Suffolk), 26
Delfont, Sir Bernard (later Lord Delfont), 142, 145
Delius, Frederick, 77
De Ramsey, 3rd Lord, 170
Derby, 17th Earl of, 98
de Vere, Robert, Earl of Oxford (later Marquess of Dublin), 27
Devonshire, 8th Duke of, 66
Devonshire, 11th Duke of, 48
Devonshire, Earl of, 23
D'Ewes, Sir Simonds, 20
Disraeli, Benjamin (later Earl of Beaconsfield), 87
Distinguished Conduct Medal, 78, 177
Distinguished Flying Cross, 82
Distinguished Flying Medal, 82
Distinguished Service Cross, 82
Distinguished Service Medal, 82
Distinguished Service Order, 79, 177
Dixie, Sir Wolstan, Bt., 56
Donaldson, Lady, G. B. E., 60
Dormer, Lord, 35
Douglas-Home, Sir Alec, Bt., *see* Home of the Hirsel, Lord
Douglas, Lord Alfred, 88
Downshire, 7th Marquess of, 48
Driberg, Tom (later Lord Bradwell), 65
Dryden, Sir Robert, Bt., 54
du Cros, Sir Arthur, Bt., 60-1
Dufferin & Ava, 5th Marquess of, 48
Dukes, precedence, 10, 11; origins, 26, 45; style, 41-2; numbers, 45; heirs, 46; Queen Victoria's views on, 47; Prince Consort's views on, 47; prospects of survival, 47, 168; wealth, 47-8
Dunedin, Viscount, 118
Durham, bishops of, 20

Earls, precedence, 10, 11; purpose, 22, 27; origins, 23, 50; creations since Life Peerage Act 1958, 41, 48; style, 41, 48; numbers, 48
Eccles, Viscount, 48, 125
Edinburgh, H. R. H. the Duke of, 43-4, 72, 75, 83
Edward II, 22, 34, 53
Edward III, 22-3, 26, founds Garter, 65
Edward IV, 31, 43
Edward VI, 22, 31
Edward VII (formerly Prince of Wales), 37-8, 46-7, bestowal of baronetcies, 57; rumour of bribes, 57-9; indiscreet letters, 60-1; bestows Garter on Lord Carrington, 66; obsession with Orders, 66; bestows Garter on Shah, 67, and Queen Alexandra, 71; founds Royal Victorian Chain, 74; founds Order of Merit, 76; 77, constitutional crisis, 94; views on socialism, 95; 99, 111-12, 127
Edward VIII (formerly Prince of Wales and later Duke of Windsor), 44, 70, 82
Edward, H. R. H. Prince, 43, 47
Elgar, Sir Edward, Bt., 74-5, 101-2
Elliot, Sir George, 88
Elizabeth I, 10, 26, 28-32, bestows Bath, 69
Elizabeth II (formerly Princess Elizabeth, Duchess of Edinburgh), 12, 42-3, creates Duke of Edinburgh a prince, 44-5; offers Churchill dukedom, 46; 64-5, patronage of Garter, 66; 68-9, admits commoner to Thistle, 69; divides Royal Victorian Order, 72; patronage of Order of Merit, 76; appoints to Privy Council, 83; Commonwealth and foreign honours, 126-7; 131-2, 137, 141, 145-9, 151, 153-5, 158-60, investitures, 161-2, 164; 165, 175-6, 178
Elizabeth the Queen Mother (formerly Lady Elizabeth Bowes-Lyon, Duchess of York and Queen Elizabeth), 68, 112, 162
Emery, Sir Peter, 140
Esquires, 27-8, 69
Essex, Earl of, 29, 31
Eure, barony of, 24
Eyres, L, 121
Ezra, Lord, 169

Fairhaven, 1st Lord, 25-6
Fairhaven, 2nd Lord, 26
Farquhar, Earl, 111-14
Field, Peggy, 142
Field, Tony, 141
Fife, 1st Duke of (formerly Earl of Fife), 46, 112, 114
Finch, Sir Thomas, 33
Fisher, Archbishop Geoffrey, 74
Fitzroy, Henry, 22
Fleming, Tom, 140
Floyer, Sir John, 57
Foot, Michael, 130, 134
Formby, George, 180
Forte, Sir Charles (later Lord Forte), 136
Francis of Teck, H. H. Prince, 126
Franks, Lord, 12, 156
Freake, C. J., 57-8
Frederick IV of Prussia, 51
Froissart, Jean, 69

Gardiner, Lord, 129
Garter, Order of, origins, 10, 65; 11, 22, 40, 44, numbers, 65, 69; patronage, 65; costume and insignia, 67-8; women admitted, 71; 162, collar days, 75; announcements of, 77; 85, 127, 132, 177
Gaunt, Prince John of, 106
Gaunt, June, 128
George I, revives Bath, 69; 85
George II, 56

187

George II, King of Greece, 105, 120
George III, creates 525 baronets, 59; founds St Patrick, 63, 86; 85
George IV (formerly Prince Regent), 55, founds St Michael & St George, 69-70; extends Bath, 86
George V (formerly Duke of York and Prince of Wales), 12, Letters Patent 1917, 43; 46, dukedom, 46-7; 51, court injunction, 61; 65, 67, accused of bigamy, 71; founds Order of the British Empire, 72-3; offer of KCVO declined, 74; 75, founds Companionship of Honour, 76; awards Order of Merit, 76, and has OM spurned, 76-7; views on socialism, 77; suggest CH for Delius, 77; accident and VC, 78; founds Military Cross, 81-2, and Military Medal, 82; admits Ramsay MacDonald to Privy Council, 82; insists on Privy Councillorship for Lord Dawson, 83; welcomes first woman privy counsellor, 83; 88-9, constitutional crisis, 94-9; 100, 103, 109-13, complains to Lloyd George, 115-16; 118, advice to MacDonald, 123-4; 159, lack of racial predjudice, 125-6; knights American, 126-7; 131, 155
George VI (formerly Duke of York), 43-5, 65, 75, and Maundy Gregory, 105, 108, 112, 119; 159
George Cross, 178
Gielgud, Sir John, 153
Gilmour, Sir Ian, Bt., 38
Glenesk, Lord, 88
Gladstone, William, 57-8, 1,000 letters to Queen Victoria on honours, 88; 91, 111, 124, 148
Gloucester, H. R. H. the Duke of, 44, 47
Goldsmith, Sir James, 142, 144-6, 149
Gormanston, 17th Viscount, 49
Grade, Sir Lew (later Lord Grade), 142, 145-6
Grafton, Duchess of, 45
Grafton, 1st Duke of, 45
Grafton, 11th Duke of, 45
Graveston, Piers, 34
Gregory, Maundy, 103, antecedents, 105; offices, 105, 108; and George VI, 105, 108, 112; and King of Greece, 105; hired by Lloyd George, 106-7; suspected of murder, 106, 121-2; police record, 108; blackmail, 108; The Ambassador Club, 108; arrest, 119; trial and imprisonment, 119, 121; death and burial of Edith Rosse, 120-22, and inquest, 121; exile and death, 122; 157
Greville, Charles, 60
Grey, Sir Edward (later Viscount Grey of Fallodon), 65
Guest, Freddy, 107
Guinness, Sir Arthur (later Lord Ardilaun), 88
Gwynn, Nell, 45

Haig, 1st Earl, 37
Haines, Joe, 146-7
Haldane, Viscount, 76
Haldane-Stevenson, the Reverend J. P., 24
Hamilton, Edward, 57-8
Hamilton, Marquess of, 42
Hamilton, William, 142
Haitink, Bernard, K. B. E., 126
Hankinson, Cyril, 71
Hanson, James, 146
Hardy, Thomas, 99
Harewood, 5th Earl of, 46
Harmsworth, Sir Hilberbrand, Bt., 111
Harris, Sir Arthur, Bt., 59
Harris, Sir Thomas, Bt., 56
Hatton, Sir Christopher, 29
Haughton, Lord, 35
Hedley-Millar, Mary, 12, 152-3
Hennessy, Peter, 12, 147
Henry III, 63
Henry IV, 69
Henry VI, 23, 31
Henry VII, 28, 31
Henry VIII, 10, bestows Garter on Henry Fitzroy, 22; 31, 95
Henry, H. R. H. Prince, Duke of Gloucester, 72
Heralds, College of, 30
Herries, Sir Michael, 161
Heath, Edward, 138-40
"Hickey, William", 148-9
Hicks, Sir Baptist (later Viscount Campden), 25
Higher Honours and Awards Committee, 154
Hillier, Dame Wendy, 153
Hodge, Sir Rowland, Bt., 109-10
Hodgkin, Dorothy, 76
Holland, Earl of, 56
Home of the Hirsel, Lord (formerly Earl of Home and Sir Alec Douglas-Home, Bt.), 49, 137-8, 169-70
Honours (Prevention of Abuses) Act 1925, 103, 117-20, 157
Hope, Bob, 126
Hotspur, Harry (Henry Percy), 106
Housman, A. E., 77
Howard of Effingham, Lord, 31
Hutchinson, George, 144-6
Hyde, (formerly the Reverend) Robert, 74

Imperial Service Medal, 162
India, Order of the Star of, 63, 72, founded, 86
Indian Empire, Order of the, founded, 86
Ingram, Arthur, 33
Investitures, 161-5
Isaccs, Sir Rufus, 71

James I, and VI of Scotland, 10, 12, bestows Garter on sons, 22; creates George Villiers Duke of Buckingham, 26; 28, 30-1, inherits throne, 32; reckless bestowal of

Index

accolade, 32-4; apologies to parliament, 33; sale of peerages, 35; founds baronetage, 53-4; sale of baronetcies, 54; arbitrates over precedence, 55; character, 56; bestowal of Bath, 69; 85, 88
James II, fn 68-9
Johnson, Samuel, 56-7
Juliana, H. R. H. Princess of the Netherlands, 68, 74
Juxon, Bishop William, fn 68

Kagan, Lord (formerly Sir Joseph Kagan), 64, 142-4, fn 145
Kelvin, Lord, 88
Kent, earls of, 20
Kent, H. R. H. the Duke of, 47, 162
Knighthood, origins of, 10, 22-3, 27-8, 63-4; 11; precedence, 21; new creations, 31-4; fines for refusing, 34; James I's creation of, 54; automatic appointments to, 60, 162; style, 65, 163; attitude of Commonwealth to, 73; clergy, 73-4; Queen Victoria's creations, 93; 20th-century creations, 93; cost of, 102, 108; George's V's views on numbers, 124; 132, awards to Tory industrialists, 135-7
Kinnock, Neil, 12, 168-9
Kipling, Rudyard, 76
Kitchener of Khartoum, 1st Earl, 25, 68, 76, 80-1
Kirkham, the Hon Pamela, 24
Knights Bachelor, Order of, 11, origins, 63, 65; insignia, 65; numbers, 131; 178
Knollys, 1st Viscount, 65-6, 95-100
Kymbe, Thomas, 43

Labouchere, Henry, 92
Labour Research Department, 135-7
Lambert, George, 90
Lanfranc, Archbishop, 22
Lansdowne, 5th Marquess of, 67
Lawrence, Sir Henry, 59
Lawson, Sir William, 90
Lee of Fareham, Lady, 126
Lee of Fareham, Lord, 126
Lennox, Charles, 22
Lennox, Duchess of, 34
Lees-Milne, James, 26, 159
Levin, Bernard, 12, 142-5
Lewis, Sir George, 99
Lewis, Kenneth, 142
Life Peers, origins, 49; numbers, 50; style, 50; George V's desire for, 96; 129-31, 171-3, 178-9
Life Peerage Act 1958, 10, 26, 40-1, 49
Lincolnshire, 1st Marquess of, 113-14
Lipton, Sir Thomas, 99
Liverpool, 2nd Earl of, 86
Livingstone, Kenneth, 38, 171
Lloyd George, David, attacks on House of Lords, 94; conflicts with Edward VII, 95; conflicts with George V, 100-3, 115-16, 124; sale of honours, 102, 108-11, 113-18, 120, 137; hires Maundy Gregory, 106-7; fall, 112, 123; sets up Royal Commission 118
London, suggested dukedom of, 46
Long, Viscountess, 39
Longford, 7th Earl of, 66, 149
Lords of Appeal, 49-50
Lords, House of, 20, 39-40, qualifications for, 41; and Life Peerage Act 1958, 49; bishops in, 50; 17th-century development of, 54; 60, introduction of new members, 75; and Great Reform Bill, 85; Conservative majority, 93-4; rejection of Home Rule for Ireland, 94, and Finance Bill, 94-5; plans to swamp, 95; attempts to reform, 95-9, 128-9, 169-70; and Parliament Act 1911, 98-9, 128; powers, 128, 130; desire to abolish, 168-9
Louis of Battenberg, H. R. H. Prince (later Marquess of Milford Haven), 48, 83
Louise, H. R. H. Princess, Duchess of Fife, 46, 112-14
Lowell, A. L., 93
Lucan, 7th Earl of, 60
Lucas-Tooth, Sir Hugh, Bt., 59
Lucas-Tooth, Sir Robert, Bt., 59
Lumley, Lord, 28

MacDonald, Ramsay, sworn privy counsellor, 82; 118, advice from George V, 123-4; refuses peerage and Thistle, 125; 131, 159
Macmillan, Harold (later Earl of Stockton), elevation, 48; maiden speech in Lords, 130; political honours, 137-8; 152, 173
Maidstone, Viscount, 34
Maidstone, Viscountess (later 1st Countess of Winchilsea), 33-4
Mar, 31st Countess of, 26
March, Earl of, 35
March & Kinrara, Earl of, 45
Margaret, H. R. H. Princess, 43, 46, 162
Margrethe II, Queen of Denmark, 68
Marie Louise, H. H. Princess, 68
Marlborough, 1st Duke of, *see* Churchill, John
Marlborough, 9th Duke of, 108
Marlborough, 11th Duke of, 172
Marlborough, dukes of, 67
Marlborough, Earl of, 29
Marquesses, precedence, 10, 26; 11, origins, 26-7; style, 41; numbers, 48; prospects of survival, 48
Mary I, 31
Mary, Queen, 73, 111, 113, 126
Mary, H. R. H. Princess, Viscountess Lascelles (later Countess of Harewood), 46
Massip, Roger, 126
Matthews, Victor (later Lord Matthews), 136

189

The Honours System

Maud, H. H. Princess, 113
Maud, H. R. H. Princess (later Queen Maud of Norway), 113
Mazzina, Peter, 108
McAlpine, Sir Robert (later Lord McAlpine), 136
McCurdy, Charles, 117
McKie, David, 141
Melbourne, 2nd Viscount, 65
Mensdorff, Count, 51
Menuhin, Yehudi, K. B. E., 126
Metcalfe, Lady Alexandra, 39
Michael of Russia, H. I. H. Grand Duke, 126
Michael of Kent, H. R. H. Prince, 43
Michael of Kent, H. R. H. Princess, 44
Military Cross, 78-82, 177
Military Medal, 82, 177
Mills, Sir John, 142
Milner, Viscount, 75
Mitchell, Austin, 12, 137
Mitchison, Naomi, 154
Monarchist League, 168
Montagu, Lord, 27
Montague, Sir Edward, 33
Montague-Smith, Patrick, 139
Moore, Henry, 77
Morley, Arnold, 90
Morrell, Lady Ottoline, 87
Mosley, Lady Cynthia, 39
Mosley, Nicholas (Lord Ravensdale), 25
Mosley, Sir Oswald, Bt., 25
Mountbatten of Burma, 1st Earl (formerly Lord Louis Mountbatten), 25, 42, 119, 127, 173
Mountbatten, 2nd Countess, 42, 173
Mountbatten, Lieutenant Philip, *see* Edinburgh, H. R. H. the Duke of
Mowbray, Segrave & Stourton, 26th Lord, 49
Muirshiel, Viscount, 49
Mulgrave, Earl of, 35
Murray, Alick, 107
Murray, Gilbert, 99
Murray, Len, 142

Naylor-Leyland, Sir Herbert, Bt., 91-2
Nelson, 1st Earl, 25
Nelson, Viscount, 24-5
Newton, Sir Isaac, 86
Nicolson, the Hon. Sir Harold, 74-5, 159
Nightingale, Florence, 76
Nolan, Sir Sidney, 77
Norfolk, dukes of, 26, 45
Northcliffe, Lord, 111
Northumberland, dukes of, 67
Northumberland, Earl of, 23

Ogilvy, the Hon. Angus, 43
Olav V, King of Norway, 74
Olivier, Lord, 77, 124, 153
Olivier, Sir Sydney (later Lord Olivier), 124

Order of Merit, 11, 66, woman admitted, 71, 76; founded, 75-6; numbers, 76; refusals, 76-7; precedence, 77; 102, 118, 132, 162, 177, 180
Ormond, 7th Marquess of, 48
Owen, David, 169
Oxford, earls of, 20, 35

Paris, Comte de, 38
Parke, Sir James (later Lord Wensleydale), 87
Parliament Act 1911, 98-9, 128
Parratt, Lady, 73
Parratt, Sir Walter, 73
Pearson, Sir Weetman (later Viscount Cowdray), 91
Peel, Sir Robert, 86, 88, fn 125
Peerage, The, 11, precedence, 21, 40, 42; inheritance, 23-6; purpose, 24-51; origins, 28, 38; increase in, 33, 50; purchase price and sales of, 35, 90-1; advantages of, 39-40; allocation of seats, 41; eligibility for parliament, 41-2; style, 41; courtesy titles, 42; Queen Victoria's views on, 47; and the Constitution, 50; income, 88; Victorian creations, 93; 20th-century creations, 93; cost of, 102, 108; 132, awards to Tory industrialists, 135-7
Peerage Act 1963, 41, 46
Peeresses in their own right, 26, 41, 87
Pembroke, Earl of, 35
Pepys, Samuel, 27
Peterborough, Bishop of, 88-9
Phillips, Mark, 43
Phillips, Percival, K. B. E., 126-7
Pine, L. G., 24
Pitt, William (the Younger), fn 125
Plummer, E. C., 121
Political Honours, 137-42, 147-8, 156-9, 168-70, 174, 178
Political Honours Scrutiny Committee, 12, 103, 118, 137, 142, 147-9, 152, 156-9, 169, 174
Pollock, Sir George, Bt., 57
Pollock, the Hon. Rosemary, 24
Ponsonby, Lady 81
Ponsonby, Sir Frederick (later Lord Sysonby), 12, 37, 73-5, 79-82, 98, 101, 112
Portal of Hungerford, 1st Lord, 25
Portland, 9th Duke of, 46
Portland, dukes of, 93
Pottinger, William, 64
Poulson, John, 64
Powell, Sir Arnold, 135
Powell, Enoch, 130
Prior, James, 139
Pritchett, Sir Victor, 153
Privy Council, 55, automatic appointments to, 82; meetings of, 82; purpose, 82-3; style, 83; Judicial Committee of, 115, 170; Gladstone's view on, 124; 131, 178

Index

Profumo, John, 83
Pym, Francis, 138

Ramsey of Canterbury, Lord (formerly archbishop of Canterbury), 74, 129
Ravensdale, barony of, 25
Rea, Lord, 147
Reeve, Henry, 60
Rice, Desmond, 11, 161-3
Richard, II, 23, 27, 53
Richard, Cliff, 140
Richmond, 1st Duke of, 45
Richmond, Duchess of, 35
Richmond & Gordon, 9th Duke of, 45
Riddell, Sir George, 88
Robarts of Truro, Lord, 34
Robertson, Sir James, 69
Robinson, Sir Joseph, Bt., 111, 114-17, 120
Rolfe, Frederick (alias Baron Corfo), 107
Romsey, Lord, 42
Roper, Sir John, 34-5
Rose, Kenneth, xii, 98
Rosebery, 5th Earl of, 90-2, 148
Rosse, Edith, 106, 119-22
Rosse, Frederick, 106
Rothermere, 1st Viscount, 101, 111
Rothschild, Baron Lionel, 88
Rowntree, Joseph, 99
Royal Victoria & Albert, 71, 86
Royal Victorian Order, 11, 65-6, origins, 70, 86; eligibility, 70-2; clergy, 74; declined, 74; announcements, 77; 102, 118, 127, 131-2, 152, 177
Royal Victorian Chain, 68, founded, 74-6; use made of by Elizabeth II, 74; 127
Rusk, Dean, K.B.E., 126
Russell, Bertrand (later 3rd Earl Russell), 99
Russell, earldom of, 163
Russell of Killowen, Lord, 163
Russell of Liverpool, 1st Lord, 163
Ruthven, 9th Lord, 74

Sackville, 4th Lord, 75
Sackville-West, the Hon. Vita (the Hon. Lady Nicolson), 46, 74-5
Saleman, Frederick, fn 122
Salisbury, 3rd Marquess of, 88-90
Salisbury, marquesses of, 67
Sankey, Sir John, 124
Scarborough, 10th Earl of, 119
Scarsdale, viscountcy of, 25
Schnedhorst, Francis, 90
Segar, Sir William, 30
Selborne, 2nd Earl of, 115
Sells, Sir David, 139
Semon, Sir Felix, 66
Shackleton, Lord, 12, 129, 156
Shaw, George Bernard, 76
Shea, Michael, 72
Shinwell, Lord, 129-30

Showering, Sir Keith, 136
Sieff, Sir Marcus (later Lord Sieff), 136
Simon, Sir John, 71
"Simple, Peter", 152
Sitwell, Sir Osbert, Bt., 152
Smith, Dodie, 153-4
Snowdon, Earl of, 43, 48
Somerset, dukes of, 22-3, 45, 47
Sysonby, Lord, *see* Ponsonby, Sir Frederick
Speed, Doris, 164-5
Spens, Lord, 41
St Albans, 1st Duke of, 44
St Aldwyn, 2nd Earl, 139-40
St Andrew's, Earl of, 47
Stanhope, Sir Philip, 35
Stanley, John, 135
Star Chamber, 29, 35
Steel, David, 12, 139, 158, 169
Stein, Sydney (later Lord Wandsworth), 90-2
Steinberg, Sir Sigmund, 142, 145
Stewart of Alvechurch, Baroness, 163
Stewart of Fulham, Lord, 163
Stewart, Sir John, Bt., 110-11
St Helier, Lady, 88
Stiffkey, Rector of, 107
St Michael & St George, Order of, 11, 40, 65, origins, 70; eligibility, 70; women admitted, 71; numbers, 131; 154, 179
Stockton, Earl of, *see* Macmillan, Harold
Stone, Sir Joseph (later Lord Stone), 146
Stonehouse, John, 83
St Patrick, Order of, 63, 68, 72, founded, 86; numbers, 86
Stuart of Wortley, Lady, 74
Suffield, Lord, 89
Summerskill, Baroness, 147-8
Sutherland, 24th Countess of, 49
Sutherland, Sir William, 103
Symonds, A. J. A., 107

Temple, Frances, 178
Tennyson, Lord, 88
Teresa, Mother, 76, 143
Thatcher, Margaret, 38, revives hereditary honours, 49, 130, 139; 59, life peers, 131, 149; withholds honours, 113-14; awards to Tory industrialists, 135-7; political honours, 137-41; personal honours list, 152-6, 159; 169, 173, 176
Thistle, Order of, origins, 10, 69; 11, 66, 68, numbers, 69; eligibility, 69; collar days, 75; 132, 162, 177
Thomas, George (later Lord Tonypandy), 49, 130
Thomson, C. B., 124
Thorneycroft, Lord, 139
Thorpe, Jeremy, 83
Traill, Lady, 39
Traill, Sir Alan, 39
Tresham, Sir Thomas, 32

191

Ulster, Earl of, 47

Vestey, Sir William, 110
Victoria Cross, 11, precedence, 77; presentation, 78; survivors, 78-9; 90, 177
Victoria, H. R. H. Princess, 113
Victoria, Queen, 44, favours dukedom of London, 46; creates Duke of Clarence & Avondale, 47-8; 51, 55, 57, 60, 67-8, Bath, 69; St Michael & St George, 70; Royal Victorian Order, 70, 72-3; Royal Victoria & Albert, 71, 86; Victoria Cross, 78-9; DCM, 79; DSO, 79; 86, Star of India, 86; Indian Empire, 86; Crown of India, 86; life peerage, 87; peeresses in their own right, 87; 88, 90, 92-4, 99, 125-6
Villiers, George (later 1st Duke of Buckingham), created, 26, 34; murdered, 34, 56; impeached, 34; sale of honours, 34-5, 55-6, 88
Viscounts, precedence, 10; 11, origins, 23; creations since Life Peerage Act 1958, 41; style, 41, 48-9; numbers, 49
von Hayek, Friedrich, 135

Wales, H. R. H. the Prince of, 43, 83, 162
Wales, H. R. H. the Princess of, 44, 47
Waite, Terry, 155
Wallace, Alfred, 77
Walsh, Pamela, 178
Warwick, Countess of, 60-1
Warwick, Earl of, 56
Watkinson, Viscount, 49
Watson, Sir Charles, Bt., 59
Watson, Sir George, Bt., 120, 122
Waugh, Evelyn, 105-6
Webb, Sidney (later Lord Passfield), 124
Wedgwood, Dame Veronica, 76
Weidenfeld, Sir George (later Lord Weidenfeld), 142-3, fn 145

Weinstock, Sir Arnold (later Lord Weinstock), 136
Wellesley, Sir Henry (later Lord Cowley), 46
Wellesley, Marquess, fn, 68-9
Wellington, 1st Duke of, 45-6, fn 68-9
Wellington, 8th Duke of, 12, 68
Westminster, Constance, Duchess of, 47
Westminster, 1st Duke of, 45, 47
Westminster, 2nd Duke of, 47
Westminster, 6th Duke of, 46-8
Westminster, dukedom of, 93
Westmorland, Earl of, 51
Whitelaw, William (later Viscount Whitelaw), 48, 130, 158
Wigram, Sir Clive (later Lord Wigram), 124-5
Wilde, Oscar, 29, 37, 107
William I, 22-3, 26, 50, 106
William II, 21
William II, Emperor of Germany, 38, 67
William IV, 85
Williams, Alan, 133
Williams, E. T., 46
Williams, Marcia (later Baroness Falkender), 141-2, 145-7
Williamson, Sir Archibald, 115-16
Williamson, James (later Lord Ashton), 90-2
Wilson, Sir Angus, 153
Wilson of Rievaulx, Lord (formerly Sir Harold Wilson), 13, breaks off talks on House of Lords reform, 41, 129; 49, 64, elevated, 134; resignation honours list, 137, 141-9, 158; political honours, 139
Wimborne, Viscount, 107
Winchester, Bishop of, 33
Winchilsea & Nottingham, 16th Earl of, 34
Windsor, Duchess of, 44-5
Windsor, Lady Ella, 43
Windsor, Lord Frederick, 43
Wynn, Sir John, 20

Yarwood, Mike, 142
Young, Hugo, 140-1